AF577101

THE LAWRENCE H. BLOEDEL COLLECTION

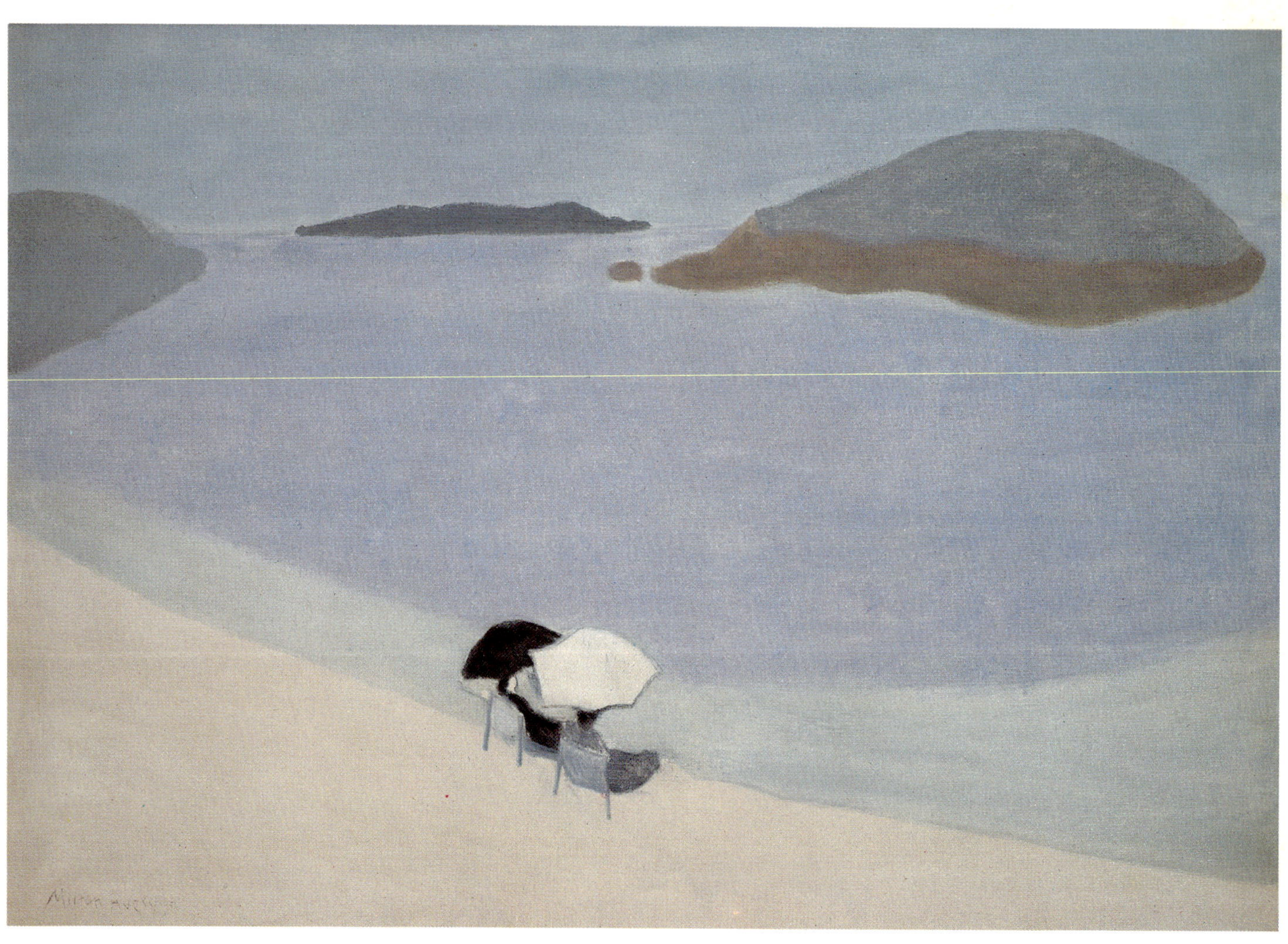

THE LAWRENCE H. BLOEDEL COLLECTION

A Loan Exhibition from the
WHITNEY MUSEUM OF AMERICAN ART
and the
WILLIAMS COLLEGE MUSEUM OF ART

Organized and Circulated by the
INTERNATIONAL EXHIBITIONS FOUNDATION
Washington, D.C.
1981–1982

Participating Museums

The Society of the Four Arts
Palm Beach, Florida

The Oklahoma Museum of Art
Oklahoma City, Oklahoma

The Arkansas Arts Center
Little Rock, Arkansas

Krannert Art Museum
Champaign, Illinois

Columbus Museum of Art
Columbus, Ohio

Seattle Art Museum
Seattle, Washington

Honolulu Academy of Arts
Honolulu, Hawaii

Trustees of the International Exhibitions Foundation

Thomas N. Armstrong, III
David Daniels
Mrs. Randolph A. Kidder
Thomas N. Maytham
Mrs. John A. Pope
Miss Alice Tully
James M. Brown, III
Mrs. Gordon P. Getty
David Lloyd Kreeger
Mrs. Constance Mellon
Robert H. Smith
Claus von Bülow
Mrs. William H. Crocker
Mrs. Prentis Cobb Hale
William S. Lieberman
David Pleydell-Bouverie
Mrs. Donald B. Straus

This project is supported by a grant from the National Endowment for the Arts (a Federal agency).
The catalogue is underwritten in part by The Andrew W. Mellon Foundation.

Copyright © 1980 by the International Exhibitions Foundation

Library of Congress Catalogue Card No. 80-83163
ISBN: 0-88397-031-7

Produced for the International Exhibitions Foundation by
The Arts Publisher, Richmond/New York

Designed by Dana Levy

Cover illustration: Cat. No. 30, Fairfield Porter, *Screen Porch*, 1964
Frontispiece: Cat. No. 1, Milton Avery, *Sea Gazers*, 1956

Acknowledgments

This exhibition from the Lawrence H. Bloedel Collection is the result of our long and fruitful collaboration with many friends and colleagues at the Whitney Museum of American Art and the Williams College Museum of Art, without whose help the project could not have been realized. First and foremost, we wish to thank Tom Armstrong, Director of the Whitney Museum and a Trustee of this Foundation, and Franklin Robinson, Director of the Williams College Museum at the time the tour was organized. Both scholars were instrumental in helping define the scope of the exhibition and in arranging the loan of the works, and we are deeply in their debt. Thanks are also due the trustees of both museums for their generosity in making these paintings available for an extended tour. At Williams College we are grateful to S. Lane Faison, Jr., Director Emeritus of the Williams College Museum for his contribution to the catalogue foreword, and to the students of the graduate seminar on American painting for their informative catalogue entries.

A very special debt of thanks is owed to Rick Stewart, Assistant Professor of American Art at Williams College, who not only selected the exhibition but also coordinated and supervised the writing of the catalogue by his graduate students. In addition, he wrote the introduction and attended to a host of practical details related to the tour, bringing to these several tasks a scholarly dedication and cheerful enthusiasm that made working with him a thoroughly enjoyable experience.

It is a pleasure to acknowledge those organizations which have provided financial assistance toward the project. The National Endowment for the Arts, a Federal agency, has given a generous grant in support of the exhibition, while the catalogue is underwritten in part by funds from The Andrew W. Mellon Foundation.

The catalogue has been produced by The Arts Publisher, Inc., with the able assistance of James Witt of that firm. We are once again grateful to Dana Levy for his thoughtful and imaginative catalogue design, and to Taffy Swandby for editing the catalogue and overseeing its production.

Finally, warm thanks are due the staff of the International Exhibitions Foundation for their untiring efforts in handling the details involved in the preparation of the exhibition, its catalogue, and its tour of seven museums.

ANNEMARIE H. POPE
President
International Exhibitions Foundation

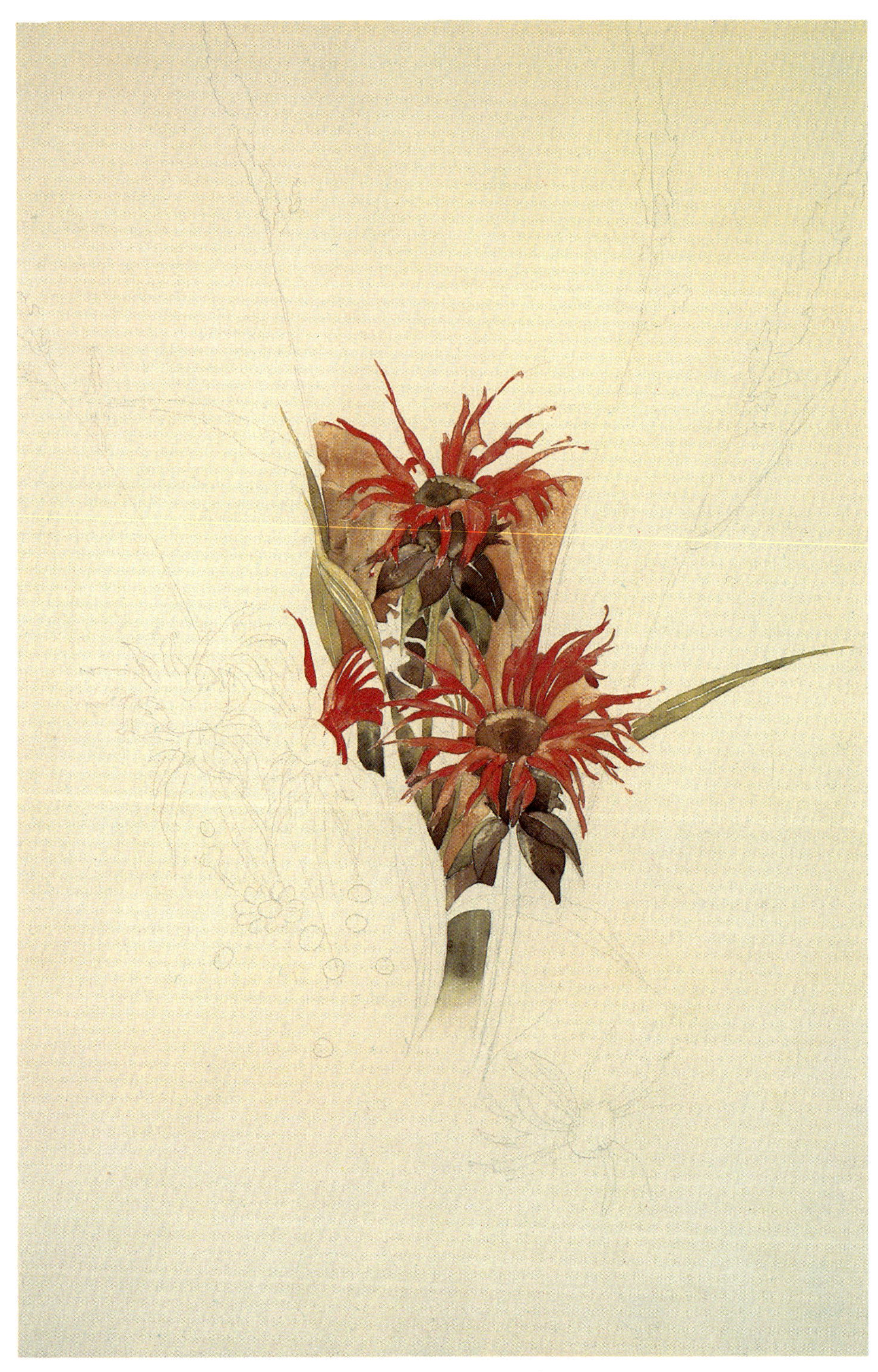

9. Charles Demuth, *Study of Bee Balm (Red Shaggy Daisies)*, c. 1923

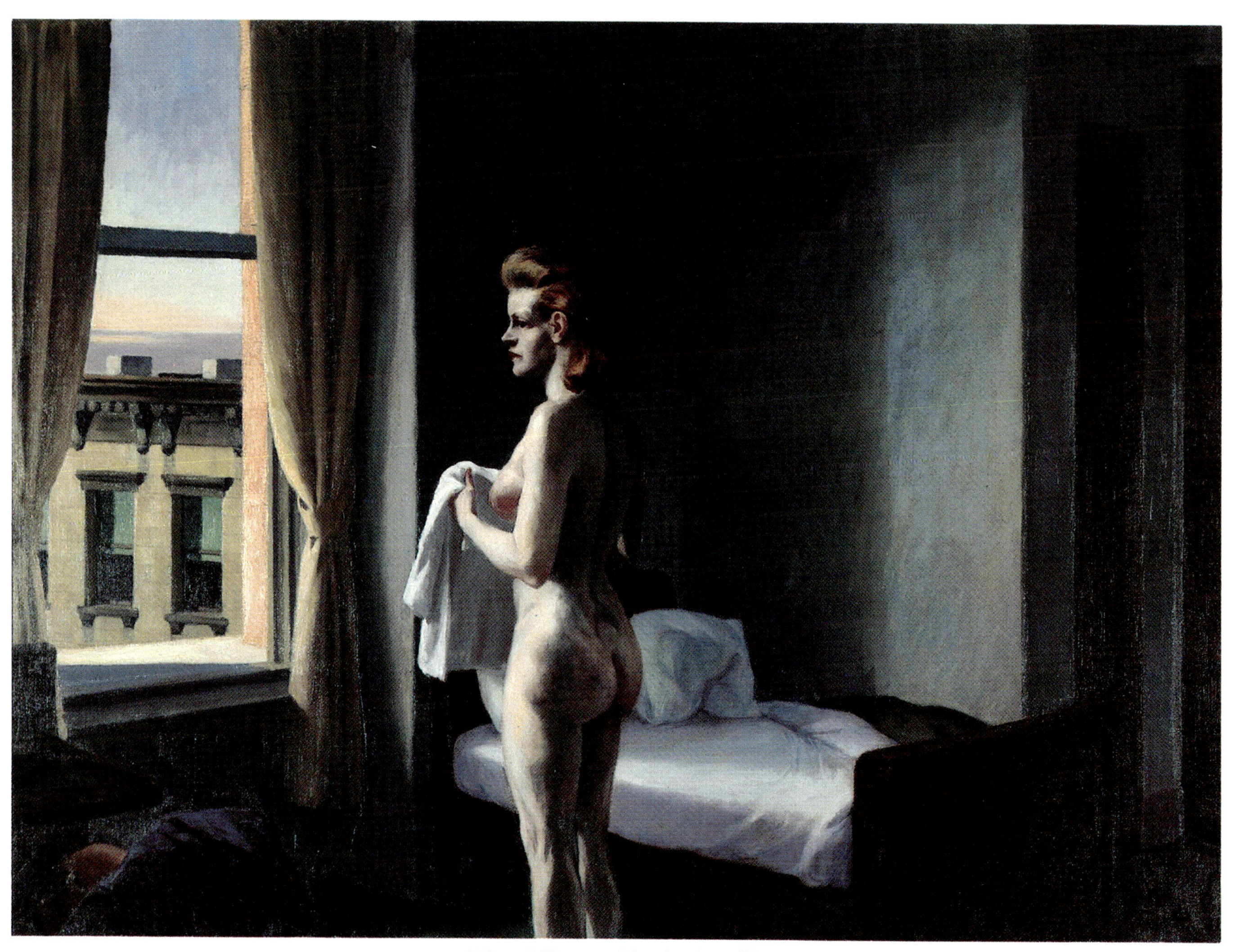

16. Edward Hopper, *Morning in a City*, 1944

Foreword

It is a great pleasure to present the finest examples from the collection of Lawrence Bloedel in a traveling exhibition which exemplifies his lifelong interest in 20th-century art and his ability to recognize quality in works by the artists he respected. The International Exhibitions Foundation is performing a great service to the public by circulating this exhibition, which provides an example of patronage and connoisseurship for those interested in the art of our country.

Lawrence Hotchkiss Bloedel was born in 1902 in Bellingham, Washington, to a family established in the lumber business. At age nine he moved with his family to Seattle; later, encouraged by his parents, he went East to attend college in Williamstown, Massachusetts. While an undergraduate at Williams College, Larry Bloedel met his future wife, Eleanore Palmedo. In 1974, Ele and Larry Bloedel celebrated their 50th wedding anniversary in Williamstown, where they had lived since 1926 and had raised their two children.

Larry Bloedel's interest in art developed after his service in the Army Ordnance Corps during the Second World War. He came to devote more and more of his time to enjoying examples of American art, which he had first begun to appreciate in college. He assembled art with a fundamental respect for the ability of the artist as a creator and innovator, often making a conscious, and characteristically anonymous, effort to encourage and support artists by purchasing their works. The Bloedels joined the Friends of the Whitney Museum of American Art in 1956 and later became Benefactors, both through their continuing generosity to all aspects of the Museum and through the Greylock Foundation, which they established in 1960 and named for the mountain they viewed each day from their home. In April 1975, Larry Bloedel became a Trustee of the Whitney Museum.

Many years ago, Larry decided that his collection should eventually be divided between the Williams College Museum of Art and Whitney Museum. Following his death in 1976, Whitney Museum curators and I visited the Bloedel homes in Williamstown and New York City to establish a list of priorities for additions to the Permanent Collection. On January 24, 1977, I met in Williamstown with the executors of Larry Bloedel's estate and representatives of the Williams College Museum of Art, then under the direction of Franklin Robinson. Frank won the toss of the coin for Williams, and he and I proceeded alternately to choose works for the two museums.

The relationship between a collector and the art collected can often become a statement of vanity by the collector. This was not the case with Larry Bloedel. His involvement with art was a personal, intimate aspect of his life which culminated in a great public gesture of generosity to a college museum and a major urban museum only after his death.

This exhibition honors Larry Bloedel and the spirit in which he pursued his interest: It illustrates, with paintings from the Bloedel Bequest to both the Whitney Museum and the Williams College Museum, how he, as a patron and private collector, has enriched the resources of these institutions and has furthered public appreciation of American art.

TOM ARMSTRONG
Director
Whitney Museum of American Art

Larry Bloedel was the ideal donor: no fuss, no vanity, and no strings attached. I shall not forget the day he came to see me and quietly announced, "Lane, you need some money for the College Museum." At the time we had under $3,000 to spend annually on purchases. His visit quintupled our purchase funds, but his donation was kept anonymous, in memory of our founder and Larry's onetime teacher, Professor Karl E. Weston. We have always been fortunate in our gifts of works of art, and had even reached the point of refusing some of them; but a new era came in with complete freedom to buy what we wanted on the Weston Fund. "Don't ask my advice," Larry said, "just go ahead on your own."

To Mr. Armstrong's accurate and perceptive remarks, little need be added except to record that in his will Larry gave two major paintings to the College Museum outright, prior to the division of his collection with the Whitney Museum. These are Edward Hopper's *Morning in a City* and Lyonel Feininger's *Mill in Autumn*—both, obviously, among our greatest American possessions. The division of the spoils was not only friendly but had its humorous moments. On both sides, rumors flew as to what the other might select, and lists slid up and down in attempts to outmaneuver. After the toss of a coin we proceeded in solemn silence through the first twenty selections. Suddenly, everyone broke out laughing, because each side had acquired nine out of ten of its top choices.

I too would like to emphasize Larry's insistence on collecting what he liked, without regard to what was fashionable in the museum world. He sought out artists who were just beginning to make their mark. Many of them later became widely recognized, but not infrequently their best work came early in their careers, and that is what Williams and the Whitney received.

There is no warmer hospitality than that of Larry and Ele Bloedel, and no warmer friendship. Blessings on them!

S. LANE FAISON, JR.
Director Emeritus
Williams College Museum of Art

Introduction

This exhibition reassembles a portion of the collection of Lawrence H. Bloedel, who bequeathed over 300 works of American art to the Whitney Museum of American Art and the Williams College Museum of Art. The Bloedel Bequest forms the nucleus of the American art study collection at Williams, and remains the third largest bequest ever given to the Whitney Museum.

Prior to the 1950s, collectors of American art were relatively few in number. Drawn from a narrow segment of the population that was comparatively affluent and well educated, there were perhaps no more than 100 scattered throughout the country. By the 1960s, however, it is estimated that the collecting public had at least doubled—an increase indicative of the general "arts explosion" of the period. At the same time, the motives for collecting shifted, or at least expanded, from a general desire to own something beautiful and lasting, to the more contemporary direction of owning something important and valuable, especially from an investment standpoint. Not surprisingly, the new American collector was apt to be from the affluent upper middle class, with newly acquired wealth that had been earned rather than inherited.

Recently it has been observed that a third generation of art collectors has emerged since the early 1970s. This group is described as being as intellectual as the first group of collectors, though not as wealthy, and as large as the second; furthermore, this group is more well informed and confident in their taste than either of the earlier two.

Lawrence Bloedel belonged in this third group in every sense. For him, collecting was such a personal matter that he avoided any lengthy commentary on it:

> My appreciation of art has always been an emotional affair rather than intellectual and my collection, such as it is, is merely an odd assortment of things that I like—things that have made such an impression on me that I felt unhappy without them. I am afraid it is in no sense an orderly or purposeful collection.

Lawrence Bloedel's interest in art collecting surfaced after World War II, when he began to purchase works by living American artists. His interest extended beyond simply collecting, however, as he made a constant effort to help support the artists from whom he bought works. From 1956 he was closely associated with the Whitney Museum of American Art, periodically serving on the committee of the collection beginning in 1959; and with his wife, Eleanore, he established the Greylock Foundation in 1960 as a beneficent enterprise for American art. Naturally, much of this was done anonymously, in the same way that he consistently and significantly aided several local arts organizations in Williamstown. By anyone's standard, Lawrence Bloedel was more than a collector of American art; he was a friend to it, despite the fact that he would probably be embarrassed to see his name mentioned so prominently in this introduction.

What of the collection, then? This exhibition is an excellent indicator of its range and complexity, and has many things to say about the development of American art in this century. One is struck by its diversity, in terms of its roots. Most of the artists exhibited came from fundamentally different backgrounds and formed their art against a backdrop of shifting artistic tastes and a basic pattern of the increasing growth and importance of art in American life. It seems obvious that Lawrence Bloedel wanted this collection to be a broad survey of American painting in the 20th century; as the entries for each work indicate, the breadth of artistic expression illustrates how very hard it can be to summarize neatly what, if anything, makes this art homogeneous, or particularly American. It is as if Mr. Bloedel wanted to make that point all along.

The nature of American painting in this century can best be indicated by utilizing a few examples from the collection. Robert Henri's *Blackwell's Island* is a fitting beginning to a period that witnessed the rise of avant-garde American painters determined to create a new art for America. Henri was at the forefront of those who believed that painting had to portray the vibrant actuality of American life. In 1908 he and his circle of artist friends would be dubbed "The Eight" for their seemingly radical beliefs, and the avant-garde scenario of artistic dissent would be fully underway. At the same time, Morton Schamberg's *Study of a Girl* gives us a different, yet equally accurate, aspect of this formative period. Schamberg was one of several young and gifted American painters who were captivated by the new modern art movements in Europe. When he painted this strong fauvist portrait after an exciting trip to Paris, Schamberg was unaware that his art would continue to transform and adapt itself to the quickening pace of the new aesthetic visions. Although he had less than ten years to live, Schamberg established himself as one of America's most important early modernists. In a sense, Henri and Schamberg represent two somewhat opposing viewpoints in the period: on the one hand, a strong figurative style that professes to draw strength from its "Americanness"; on the other, an art that insists on a fusion of European and American elements in order to achieve a higher form of expression. These views, one national, the other international, were to clash more than once in the course of the century.

The decade surrounding World War I saw great progress in modern painting. The works in the exhibition by Konrad Cramer, Max Weber and Morgan Russell illustrate the range of adaptation and interpretation that American painters of the period brought to seminal movements like Cubism, Futurism and Orphism. Cramer's *Improvisation 1* shows how quickly the influence of Kandinsky and the Munich school penetrated the American avant-garde circles; Weber's *Draped Female Nude and Sleeping Child* demonstrates that he was one of the most prolific and successful of the American cubists; Russell's *Synchromy #6*, though not painted until the early twenties, exemplifies the Synchromist movement which in 1913 proclaimed the superiority of color abstraction and represented the first such modern movement in American painting. Experimentation flourished, and John Marin's *Stonington Maine*, with its somewhat abstract treatment of a traditional subject, reveals the extent to which the modernist vision permeated the art of even the more established painters of the time. In the end, the most original artists exhibited not a particular style as much as a new aesthetic latitude, a new way of perceiving their world.

American painters were convinced, in the decade or so following the war's end, that art was one of the few ways out of the socio-political quagmire that had cost so many lives and undermined so many values. One clear manifestation of this general belief was a sharp turn towards representative American subject matter, rendered with an eye accustomed to the modern styles. Joseph Stella's *Brooklyn Bridge* was seen as an icon to things American, just as it was to be for Hart Crane a few years later. In the same way, Charles Demuth's small and intimate watercolors proclaim a new Walden, a sense of rediscovery of America's microcosm that his friend, the poet William Carlos Williams, aggressively touted as the "local" vision, the only one that could work for American artists.

This attitude may explain why so many painters in the 1930s and 1940s created such powerful yet personal visions of the American scene. Like Walt Whitman, whom they took as their fountainhead, these artists were celebrators of American life who brought to their art a strong sense of the creative individual. Edward Hopper's *Morning in a City* and Charles Sheeler's *On a Connecticut Theme* present their subjects in a straightforward way, but the images they evoke are highly complex and very personal. Both paintings stimulate the viewer's interest in the relationship between a person and his environment, and the discovery of this relationship is brought about by means of a heightened, rarified perception. Here the artist is not an interpreter; he is a guide.

Lawrence Bloedel preferred works that continued this tradition. Paintings by Milton Avery, Richard Diebenkorn, Fairfield Porter and others in the exhibition fully explore issues that have existed for American art throughout this century. In these works one sees a vindication of the two different but equally significant directions indicated by Henri and Schamberg more than seventy years ago. The view of these artists is American by virtue of their subject matter, but their vision is wholly modern and transcends the often mundane people and their surroundings. The subjects in Porter's *Screen Porch* exist in our own time, but are rendered beyond it. In a tribute to Porter, the poet John Ashbery wrote:

> This is perhaps the lesson of his painting too: that there are no rules or anything, no ideas in art, just objects and materials that combine, like people, in somewhat mysterious ways . . . that we are left with our spontaneity and that life itself is a series of improvisations during the course of which it is possible to improve on oneself but never to the point where one doesn't have to improvise. ("Four Tributes," *Art in America*, 61, Jan–Feb 1976, p. 20)

Perhaps this is the lesson Lawrence Bloedel wished to convey in his lifetime of collecting; that for all of us, in Porter's own words, "a painting is a fact, arbitrary and individual." So it appears to be in this exhibition.

Lawrence Bloedel would have been pleased to know that this catalogue is almost entirely the work of students. In the fall of 1978 a Williams College seminar on American painting of the 20th century, held in the graduate art history program at the Sterling and Francine Clark Art Institute, embarked on this project, and without the participants' dedication and enthusiasm this catalogue would not have been possible. The students were Cheryl Brutven, Kathleen Burnside, Hiram Butler, Laurie Crichton, Laura Giles, Joellen Harrison, Laurie Jones, Franklin Kelly, Gwendolyn Owens, Ann Silvi, Mary Spivy, Barbara Tipping, Louise van Dyck and Jennifer Wade. In January 1979, Laurie Crichton was killed in an automobile accident and the field of art history lost a promising young scholar in the history of textiles. It is her fellow students' wish that their efforts for this catalogue be dedicated to her memory.

Since Mr. Bloedel bequeathed half of his collection each to the Whitney Museum and the Williams College Museum of Art, this exhibition would have been completely unmanageable without close cooperation between the two institutions. Thomas Armstrong, Director of the Whitney, and Patterson Sims, Associate Curator of the collection, went out of their way to be helpful and patient when an unwieldy group of students visited the museum to study the Bloedel works and subsequently peppered the museum with individual queries. Anita Duquette, Registrar of the museum, handled a vast number of administrative details and deserves sincere thanks.

Franklin W. Robinson, then Director of the Williams College Museum, sparked the initial idea for the exhibition, and John W. Coffey, his successor, saw it through with his customary dedication and efficiency, capably assisted by Museum Secretary Libby Kieffer. In the course of researching and writing the catalogue the students were afforded an invaluable lesson in the mechanics of preparing a large-scale exhibition for travel, and I am happy to report that well over half of their number are now actively pursuing related careers in the arts.

The Williams College Museum is extremely grateful to the National Endowment for the Arts and to the Massachusetts Council for the Arts and Humanities for matching grants which enabled nearly all of its share of the exhibition to be properly cleaned and restored so that they could be seen to best advantage. The Williamstown Regional Conservation Laboratory, under the direction of Gerald Hoepfner, carried out all the work with the greatest skill and deepest interest.

Finally, this exhibition has been organized by the International Exhibitions Foundation, an organization of which Lawrence Bloedel knew and doubtless approved, since its purpose is the dissemination of art to broad geographic areas as a learning experience. Mrs. John A. Pope, Director of the Foundation, guided the exhibition from the very beginning and supported the efforts of the class at crucial stages. Taffy Swandby, the Foundation's editor, suffered innumerable delays in the production of the catalogue in order to refine the finished product, and I owe her a special debt of gratitude.

Though I never knew Lawrence Bloedel, I can't help but feel that he would have given enthusiastically of his time to help the students prepare this catalogue. One of his main desires undoubtedly was to see his collection inspire and instruct; in no small way, this exhibition realizes that desire, and thereby serves as the best kind of memorial to him.

RICK STEWART

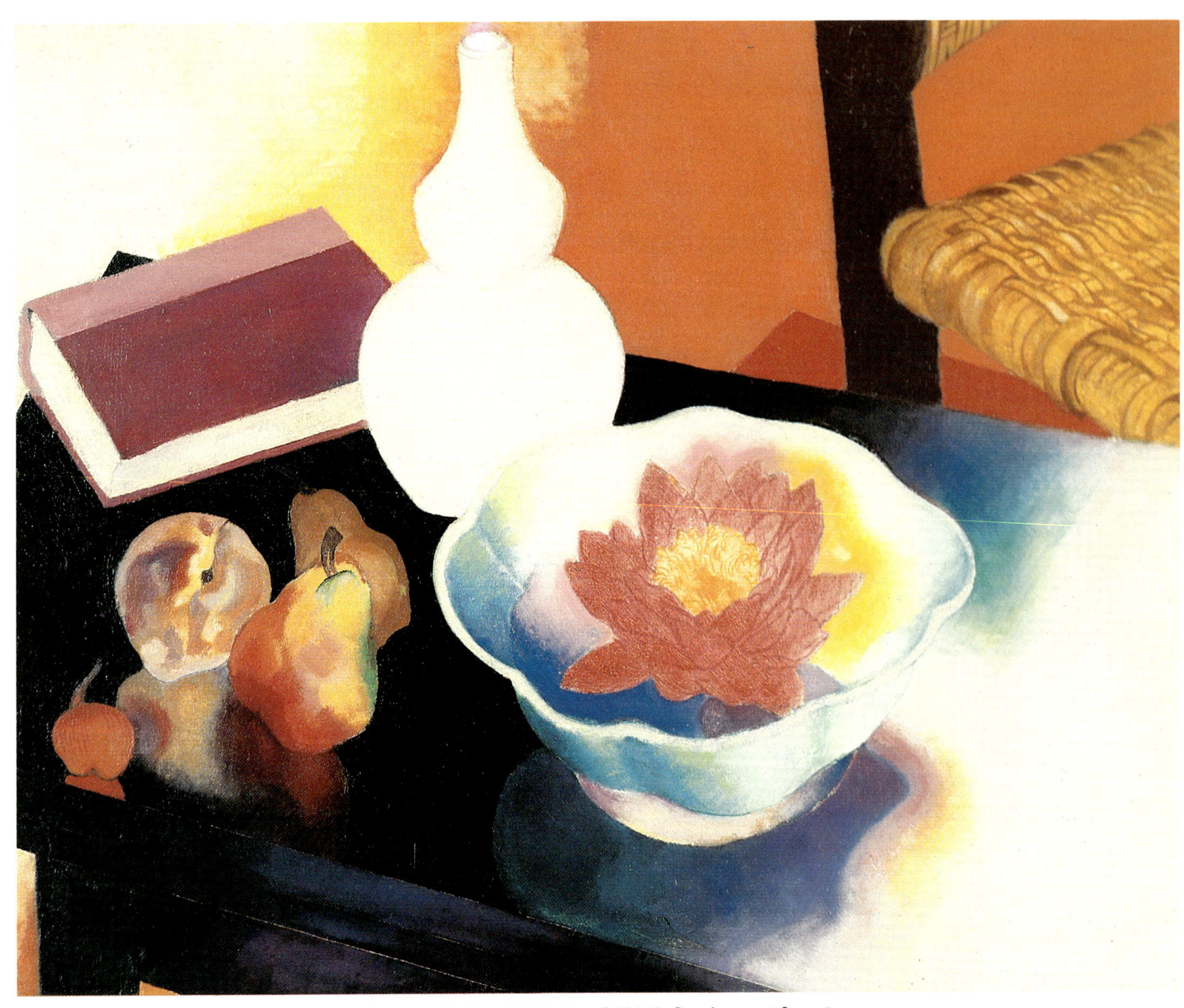

20. Stanton MacDonald-Wright, *Still Life Synchromy #3*, 1928

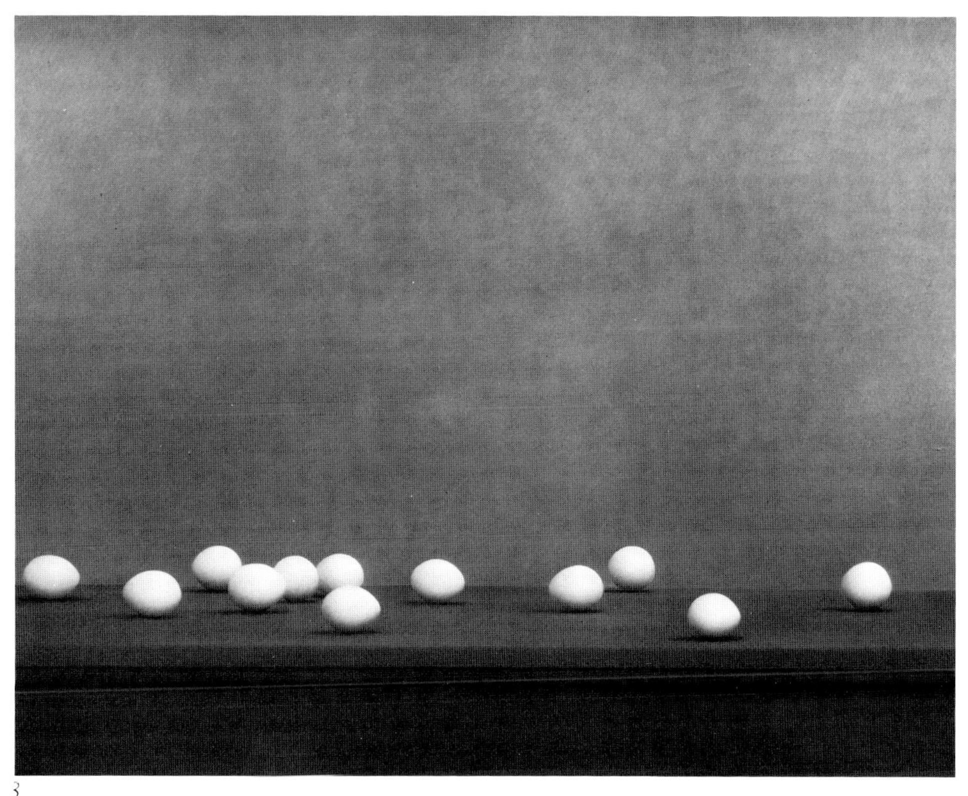
3

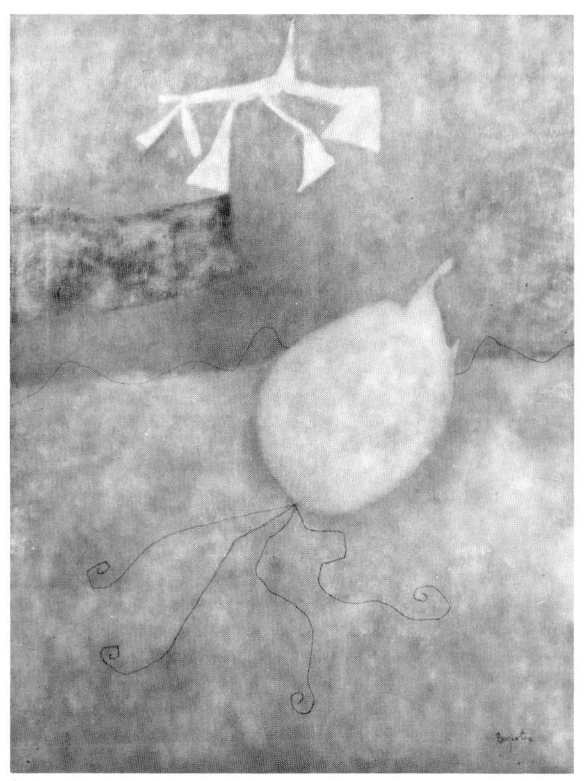
4

gaze for a long time at the bottom of a still pond" (quoted in "William Baziotes," *Location*, vol. 51, no. 2, p. 89). *Sand* may be just such a soothing symbol, with its liquid shapes and bleached colors, but the calm is not complete. Throughout his life Baziotes was intrigued with the relationships between the known and the unknown, and good and evil. In *Sand* a spiked form floats near a rounded balloon-like shape, suggesting the possibility of danger. The spidery legs are both extraordinarily delicate and suggestive of some strange creature. The shapes and colors of this picture owe something to Baziotes' habit of inspecting the collection of bones and shells at the American Museum of Natural History.

The element of mystery found in *Sand* is not unusual in the works of Abstract Expressionists. Like some of his contemporaries, Baziotes had faith in autonomous painting and sought his subconscious, encouraging the unknown self to take over the canvas. He described the process: "Each beginning suggests something. Once I sense the suggestion I begin to paint intuitively. The suggestion then becomes a phantom that must be caught and made real. As I work, or when the painting is finished, the subject reveals itself" (Baziotes, "I Cannot Evolve any Concrete Theory . . ." *Possibilities*, no. 1, winter 1947/48, p. 2).

J. W.

Cavaliere, Barbara. "An Introduction to the Method of William Baziotes."*Arts Magazine*, vol. 51, no. 8, April 1977, pp. 124–31.

Hadler, Mona. "William Baziotes: A Contemporary Poet Painter." *Arts Magazine*,vol. 51, no. 10, June 1977, pp. 102–111.

Preble, Michael. *William Baziotes: A Retrospective Exhibition*. Newport Beach, California: Newport Harbor Art Museum, 1978.

William Baziotes, A Memorial Exhibition. New York: The Solomon R. Guggenheim Museum, 1965.

ELMER NELSON BISCHOFF (b. 1916)

5. COUNTRY ROOM, 1957

Oil on canvas
48⅞ x 57½ (124.1 x 146.0 cm.)
Signed and dated on verso: *Elmer Bischoff 3/57*
Williams College Museum of Art

Elmer Nelson Bischoff, born in 1916, completed his studies in studio art and received his M.A. in 1939 from the University of California at Berkeley. He began a career in education soon after, leading in 1946 to the California School of Fine Arts, where he served as Chairman of the Graduate Department from 1959 to 1962. Bischoff's style of painting evolved from an adherance to Cubist tendencies to working within the Abstract Expressionist mode. His development toward a representational image was realized after a temporary, self-imposed isolation and his resignation from teaching in order to spend more time painting. Participation in group shows and continuous work led to the Oakland presentation where the "figurative abstractionists" were first seriously examined as a new "school."

In *Country Room*, specific emotional responses are evoked by the artist's choice of composition, color and manner of depicting a rather ordinary subject. Bischoff has maintained his early technique of paint application; severe, defined strokes with a loaded brush create a surface which is obviously expressive and as important as the subject. As he did in most of his other work during this period, Bischoff has here portrayed the figure in an anonymous manner. Despite the absence of individual characteristics, Bischoff successfully calls up emotions by means of the severe lighting, pose and gesture of the figure within the austere room. His colors emphasize the solitude of the figure, who seems to ignore the lush world visible through the entrance. Figurative Abstractionists like Bischoff were often criticized for a "meaningless imagery" dominated by technique. Yet Bischoff maintained this style until 1972, when his work drastically changed to an almost Surrealist imagery painted in acrylics rather than oils.

C.B.

Curtis, Cathy. "Elmer Bischoff: Ties to the Landscape." *Artweek* (Oakland), vol. 10, no. 18, 5 May 1979, p. 7.

Kramer, Hilton. "Month in Review: Elmer Bischoff and the San Francisco School of 'figuratives'." *Arts*, vol. 34, no. 4, January 1960, pp. 42–45.

St. John, Terry. *Elmer Bischoff: Figurative Paintings 1957–1972*. Oakland Museum of Art, 1975.

JAMES BROOKS (b. 1906)

6. HANRAHAN, 1966

Acrylic on canvas
36 x 43 (91.4 x 109.2)
Signed lower right: *J. Brooks*; dated on verso, *1966*
Whitney Museum of American Art

James Brooks moved to New York from Dallas in 1926, to study at the Art Students League. His murals painted for the W.P.A. between 1936 and 1942 have been seen as some of the best executed under that project. After World War II, Brooks painted in a synthetic Cubist idiom; his painting

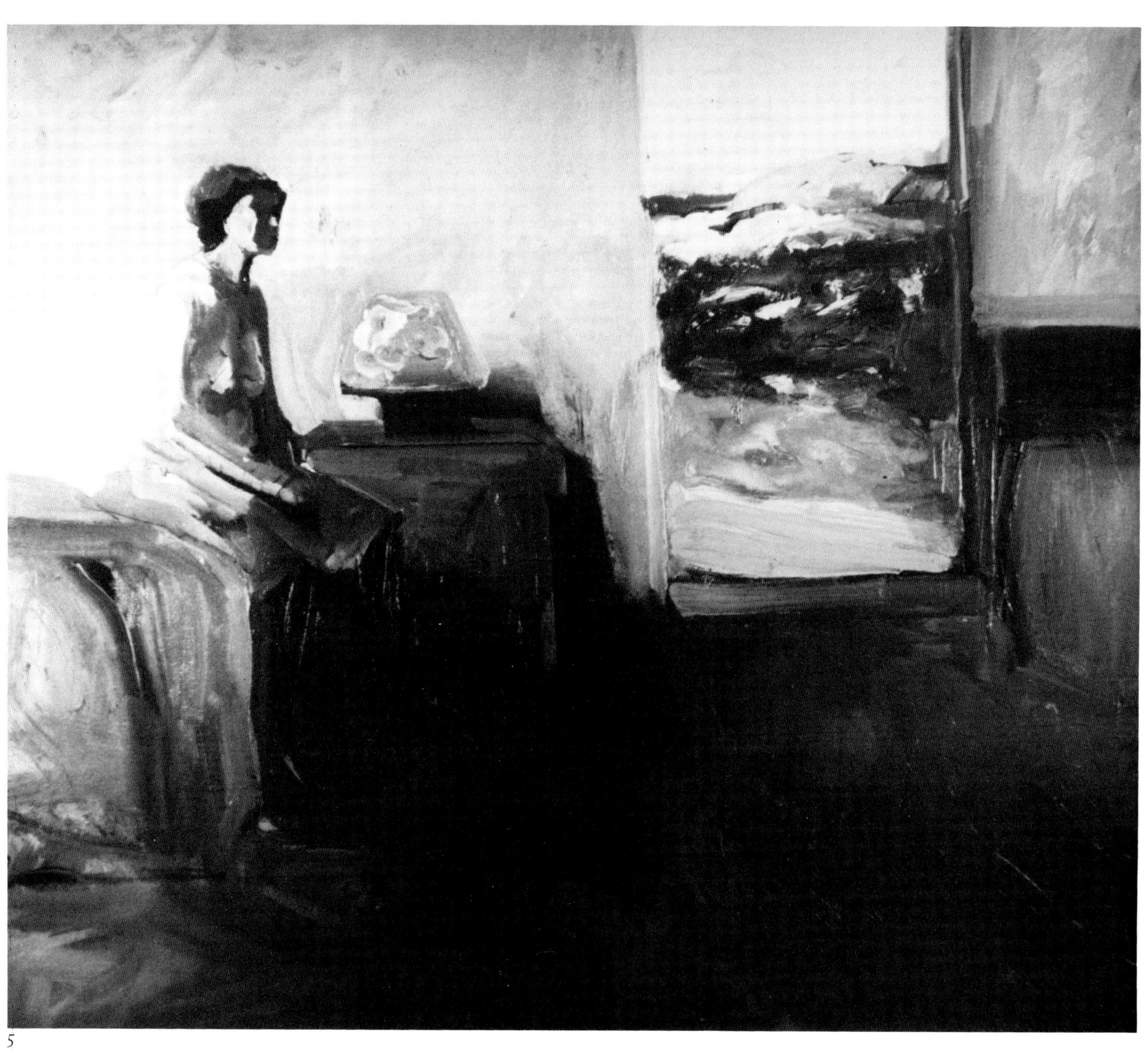

5

became consistently freer and looser. In 1946 he saw much of Jackson Pollock, and while he learned from him, he nonetheless created a form of abstraction that was much less aggressive and more lyrical than that of Pollock.

After 1948 Brooks began to experiment and paint more freely. He glued paper to canvas and used the forms made by glue showing through the paper as part of his composition. The following year he poured paint on the back of an absorbent canvas so that it soaked through, creating "accidental" areas of color which were then incorporated into the composition of the painting (Sandler, p. 233). This predates by three years Helen Frankenthaler's famous staining in *Mountains and Sea* (Ratcliff, p. 146). However, Brooks did not continue, with this surface painting. During the 1950s he reintroduced Cubist structures similar to those in his pre-1947 paintings (Sandler, p. 234). By the early 1960s, Brooks was using what appear to be large calligraphic motifs on a heroic scale which retained an active and heavily modulated surface. After 1965, he incorporated some of the more impersonal art currents of the decade and moved away from Expressionist brushwork.

Hanrahan, painted in 1966, demonstrates Brooks' late style. Large indistinct areas of pure color float across the seemingly unbounded field of the painting. Thin curved lines accent these areas like tentative gestures, giving a lighter, more whimsical aspect to the work. In *Hanrahan,* the calligraphy and lyricism of Brooks' earlier works have been transposed into a broader, more heroic statement.

H.B.

Hunter, Sam *James Brooks.* New York: Whitney Museum of American Art, 1963.

"James Brooks." *Magazine of Art,* vol. 46, no. 1, January 1953, pp. 24–25.

Ratcliff, Carter. "The Paintings of James Brooks." *Arts Magazine,* vol. 53, no. 1, September 1978, pp. 145–147.

Sandler, Irving. "James Brooks and the Abstract Inscape." *Art News,* vol. 61, no. 10, February 1963, pp. 30–31.

EDWARD CORBETT (1919–1971)

7. PROVINCETOWN, SEPTEMBER 1963, #2, 1963

Oil on canvas
48 x 40 (121.9 x 101.6)
Unsigned
Whitney Museum of American Art

A member of a nomadic military family, Edward Corbett first studied art at the Dayton Art Institute in 1932. Five years later, study at the California School of Fine Arts exposed him to Cézanne and the French Cubists. After a stint in the Merchant Marine during World War II, Corbett went to New York City, where he was immediately captivated by the work of Mondrian. He moved to San Francisco in 1947 to begin a career in teaching, and there became deeply involved with existentialism. He evolved an expressive style of painting, made up of nonobjective forms floating on a limitless dark background—a style that doubtless owed its existence to the dominating presence of Clyfford Still in the Bay Area in the same period.

In the early 1950s Corbett spent a brief period in Mexico, during which he virtually ceased to paint; but his inclusion in the Museum of Modern Art's *15 Americans* show in 1951 ended this hiatus. As a result of this exposure Corbett was offered a long-term teaching position at Mt. Holyoke College in South Hadley, Massachusetts.

With his position secure, Corbett began to evolve a key series of paintings which he called "paintings for Puritans," consisting of layers of carefully built-up paint, white on white. The surfaces of these works barely concealed myriad traces of color and shadow, as if the artist wanted to emphasize the silent complexity of the creative process. *Provincetown, September 1963, #2,* belongs to the period immediately following the white-on-white works; like them, it is a lyrical work made up of soft, broken planes of glazed color, floating against an indistinct background. These shapes appear to settle into a vague landscape, but the sense is that it is more of a landscape of the mind. Corbett wrote of his intention in paintings such as this: "I hope to do works which give the viewer the emotion of waiting, not the experience of possessing an event, but a mystery in his mind about what might happen" (Nordland, p. 21). Such qualities are certainly evident in *Provincetown, September 1963, #2;* we wait, unsure of ourselves, in an atmosphere of expectation.

R.S.

Nordland, Gerald. *Edward Corbett.* University of Maryland Art Gallery, College Park, 1979.

Ashton, Dore. "The San Francisco School." *Evergreen Review,* no. 2, 1957, pp. 148–159.

Miller, Dorothy, ed. *15 Americans.* New York: Museum of Modern Art, 1952.

KONRAD CRAMER (1888–1963)

8. IMPROVISATION #1, 1912

Oil on canvas
29 ¾ x 24 (75.6 x 61.0)
Signed and dated lower right: *K. Kramer 1912*
Whitney Museum of American Art

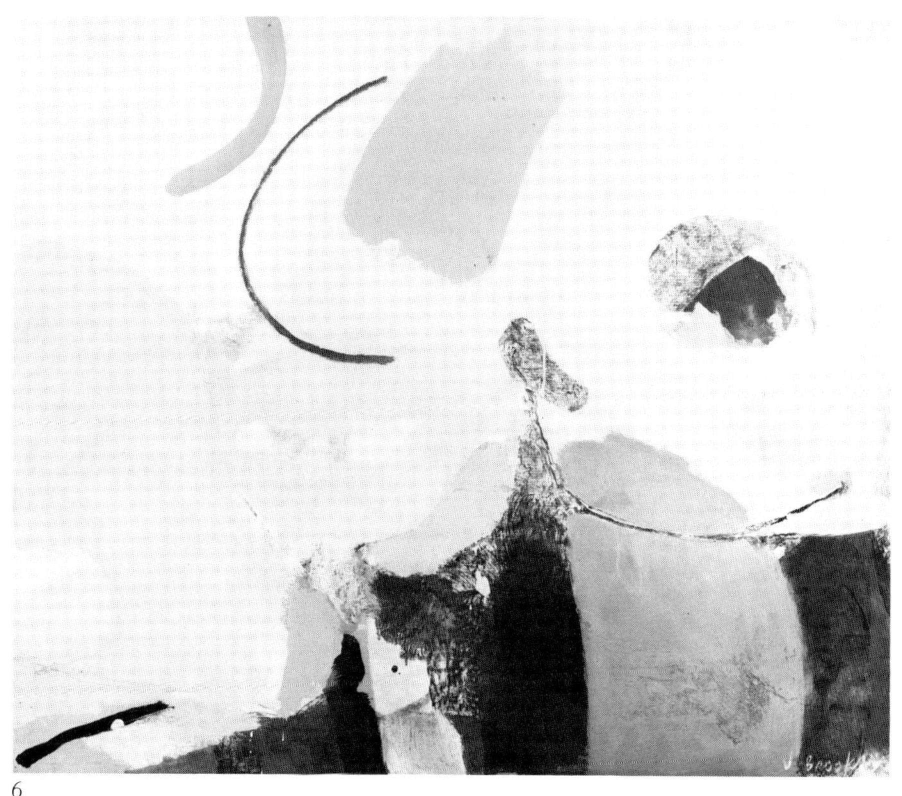

6

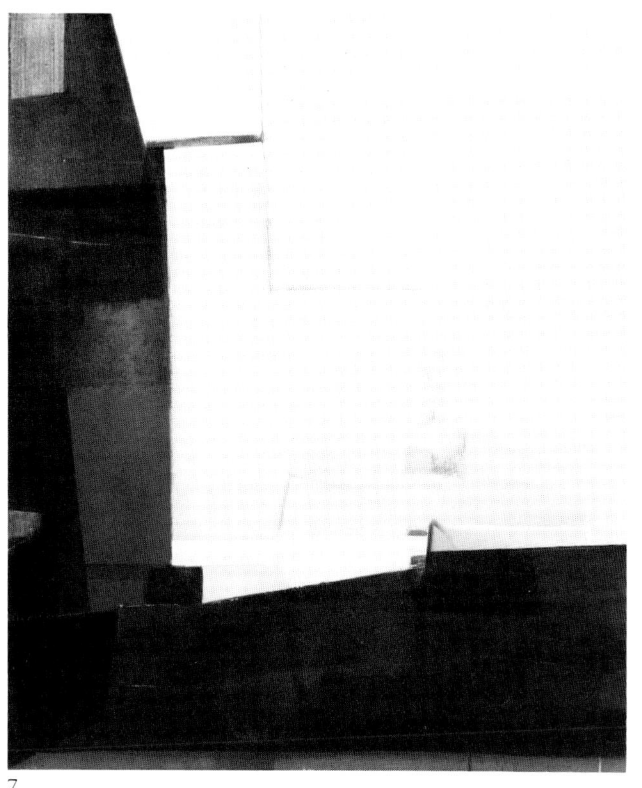

7

Born in Würzburg, Germany, in 1888, Konrad Cramer began his studies at the Academy of Fine Arts in Karlsruhe before going in 1910 to Munich. There, Wassily Kandinsky and Franz Marc were formulating their revolutionary ideas concerning the expression of an inner spiritual reality in painting by means of color and form. Upon Cramer's arrival in Munich, Kandinsky was already presenting "improvisations" that, like Marc's compositions, remained tied to recognizable imagery before evolving into complete abstractions a few years later. In Cramer's *Improvisation #1*, the abstract composition, brilliant color scale and broad, repetitive brushstrokes show similarity to works by Kandinsky and Marc. The actual composition, with its tight, sweeping movement composed of severe curved and triangular elements, is closer to Marc's work despite Cramer's gravitation, by 1913, towards work remarkably similar to that of Kandinsky.

In 1911 Cramer came to the U.S. with his new bride, Florence Ballin, an American student whom he met in Munich. Both became involved in the contemporary art world, dividing their time between the artists' colony of Woodstock and New York City. Cramer's awareness of the European avant-garde made inevitable his contact with "291" and Alfred Stieglitz, as well as his close friendship with the American painter Andrew Dasburg, who had been exposed to the American Synchromists in Europe and who carried on with Cramer an extensive dialogue concerning color charts and chromatic scales. In 1913 the two artists exhibited together in a group show, Cramer's first in this country, at the Macdowell Club of New York City. *Improvisation #1*, which reflects the general concerns of Dasburg and the movement, may well have been one of the six "improvisations" by Cramer included in the show.

In recent years, Konrad Cramer's importance as one of the most original artistic innovators in the Stieglitz circle has been verified by historians. *Improvisation #1* is clear evidence that early modernism in American art was not solely dependent, as is often believed, on developments emanating from Paris. Rather, artists like Cramer drew equally from what they understood to be happening in Germany, especially the Blaue Reiter circle and its accomplishments in art and theory. When a fuller understanding of this crucial period is realized, Konrad Cramer will take his place as a leading artistic innovator.

Archives of American Art, Konrad Cramer papers, reel D 171.

Avant-Garde Painting and Sculpture in America 1910–25. Wilmington: Delaware Art Museum and the University of Delaware, 1975.

Levin, Gail. *Synchromism and American Color Abstraction 1910–1925.* New York: Whitney Museum of American Art, 1978.

CHARLES HENRY BUCKIUS DEMUTH (1883–1935)

9. STUDY OF BEE BALM (RED SHAGGY DAISIES), c. 1923

Watercolor and pencil on paper
16 ½ x 11 (41.9 x 27.9)
Unsigned
Williams College Museum of Art

10. JACK-IN-THE-PULPITS, c. 1920–21

Watercolor over graphite
Irregular oval: 13 ¾ x 10 (34.9 x 25.4)
Unsigned
Williams College Museum of Art

Born in Lancaster in 1883, Charles Demuth attended the Pennsylvania Academy of Fine Arts, where he studied under Thomas Anshutz and William Merritt Chase. In 1904 and 1907, and again at the end of World War I, Demuth visited Paris, where he likely saw Cubist works by Picasso, Braque and Picabia, and certainly absorbed the modernist atmosphere. He became another member of the group of American artists living and working in Paris that included John Marin, Arthur Dove and Marsden Hartley.

Upon returning to the States in 1914, Demuth entered into the avant-garde milieu of artists and intellectuals in New York City. His love for flowers surfaced in the early teens in works with broad washes, dark backgrounds and bright bouquets. The year 1916 was a crucial one stylistically, as Demuth traveled to Bermuda, almost certainly with Marsden Hartley, and painted Cubist-inspired landscapes. Upon his return he developed his own brand of Cubist-Realism into a precise and selective vision of the world, whether it be manifested in a small still life or one of his temperas of industrial and architectural inspiration. A diabetic condition caused Demuth's death in 1935, but not before he had received considerable recognition among artists and critics of his day, showing at the Daniel Gallery and Alfred Stieglitz's Intimate Gallery.

In his time, Demuth was largely known for his accomplished and delicate still-life flower and fruit pieces of the 1920s. *Jack-in-the-Pulpits* is a small (13 ¾ x 10") oval watercolor which presents an ambiguous combination of forms and expressive, blotted washes of primarily dark and subtle hues. Wine-brown blossoms of some intensity stand out in the work to the

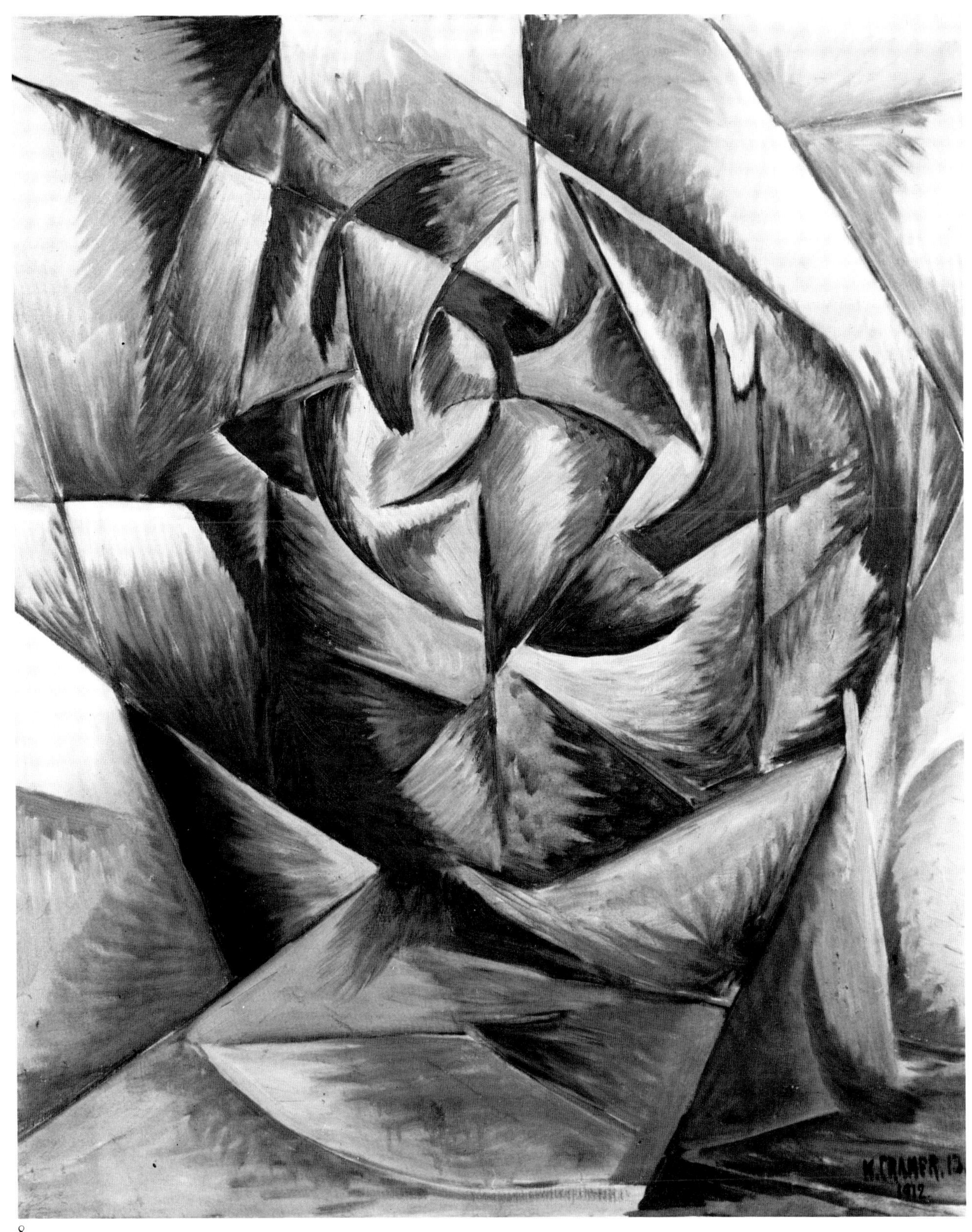

8

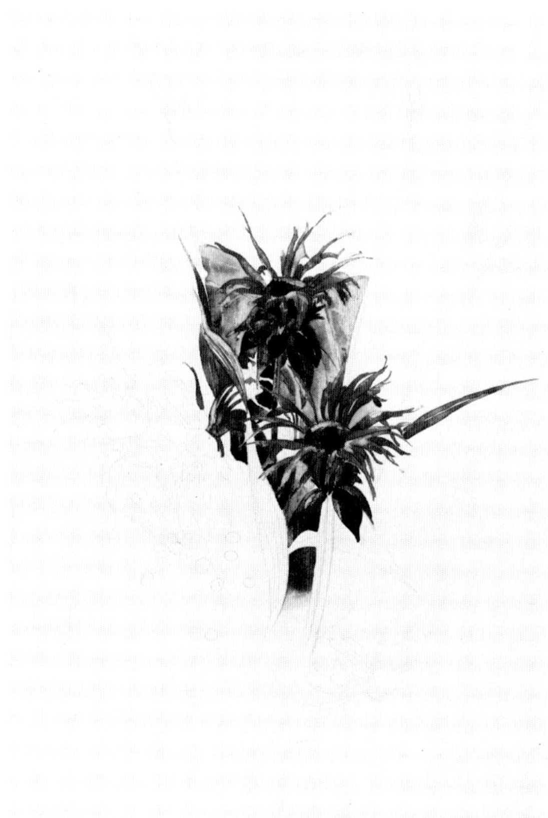

9

left of center. Demuth conceives his composition carefully, with particular attention to the formal interaction of parts. He creates an image which seems to evolve from a main "root." He then manipulates this image with wash as well as with linear modifications to create a highly suggestive though ambiguous sensation of three dimensionality. Stems of the foreground adapt their color in relation to the hues which surround them. The grey washes (indicated) of the background are not easily read, but they echo and even extend the curvilinear qualities which Demuth so carefully pencils in below. In other words, Demuth is constantly trading off pictorial Realism and the illusion of depth for purely coloristic and linear concerns. His statement here, much like his personality, is oblique rather than direct.

Jack-in-the-Pulpits, although unsigned and undated, is regarded by Emily Farnham in her catalogue raisonné as having been painted c. 1920–21. In support of this thesis she cites a general classification of works done in these years as "oval vignette compositions." However, one might argue with some justification that this work has typical elements of the late Demuth watercolor.

In contrast to the quietude of *Jack-in-the-Pulpits*, *Study of Bee Balm* is a piece brimming with vitality, sparkling colors and deft strokes. It, too, is a watercolor and pencil composition, unsigned and undated. Generally regarded as unfinished, it has been linked to two other works as part of *Still Life: Three Studies*. *Study of Bee Balm* blooms into a marvelous V-shaped bouquet, with flowers set off against the stark white paper. The clarity of form, the purity of color, the swift hard-edged strokes make this work more readable than *Jack-in-the-Pulpits*. Additionally, the painting has a spontaneous naturalness; it seems more a work of immediate perception, less of a carefully hewn ambiguous symbol.

The period from 1923 to 1926 is what Emily Farnham calls Demuth's period of the V-shaped still-life composition. Yet the clean, sharp edges and the sense of selectivity also remind one of the period 1927–29 when Demuth was continually reducing, simplifying and sharpening his vision of the world. Although Farnham calls these works "laborious" and "technically dry," one could argue that the life in this precise vision comes by virtue of its being a study and may indeed have been painted as late as 1929.

These two still-life compositions, as most of this genre in Demuth's work, show only a suggestive and modified view of Cubist theory. There is a subtle reshifting of objects and colors, sometimes at the expense of traditional pictorial depth, to create a faceted and complex image of the flowers. Yet there is no comprehensive analysis of forms with the purpose of combining a multitude of views of the object. It is likely that Cézanne's still lifes served as a model for Demuth in his choice to retain a traditionally realistic image in spite of some formal manipulation and innovation. In this genre, the avant-garde tradition which he takes up allows him to be playful, suggestive and even oblique while purifying and aestheticizing his cherished Lancaster flowers. And in the midst of his more purposely abstract works, these still lifes mediate between the modern and the traditional.

K.B.

Farnham, Emily. "Charles Demuth." Unpublished Ph.D. dissertation, Ohio State University, 1959.

Gebhard, David and Phyllis Plous. *Charles Demuth: the mechanical encrusted on the living*. University of California, 1971.

Hartley, Marsden. "Farewell Charles." *The New Caravan*. New York: W. W. Norton, 1936.

McBride, Henry. "Watercolors by Charles Demuth." *The Studio*, no. 22, 1929, pp. 634–35.

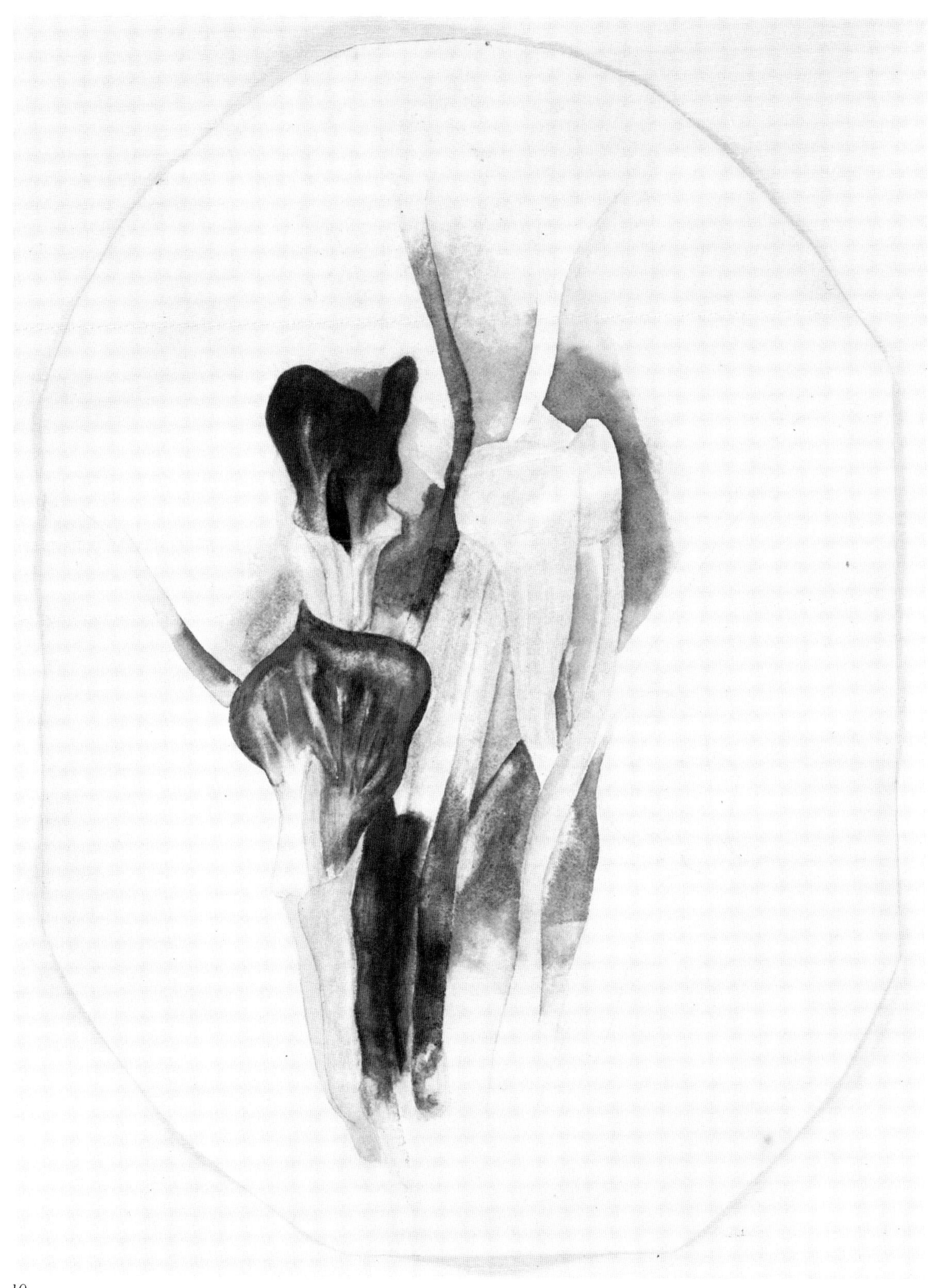

10

RICHARD DIEBENKORN (b. 1922)

11. BATH, 1960

Oil on canvas
66 x 61 1/4 (167.7 x 155.6)
Signed and dated lower right: *RD60*
Williams College Museum of Art

Richard Diebenkorn is perhaps the most celebrated contemporary artist from the western United States. He studied painting for several years and graduated from Stanford University in 1943. While there he had been impressed with Edward Hopper's American imagery; he also saw works by Matisse, Picasso and Cézanne in the home of Sarah Stein. While serving in the Marine Corps in North Carolina, Diebenkorn became further acquainted with works by these artists by visiting the Phillips Collection in Washington, D. C. He later returned to San Francisco and enrolled in the California School of Fine Arts. The faculty included not only Elmer Bischoff and David Park, but the New York artists Clyfford Still, Mark Rothko and Ad Reinhardt, who were visiting faculty members. The summer of 1953 was spent in New York, where Diebenkorn met Franz Kline and saw Willem de Kooning's work. He then returned to California to teach at the California College of Arts and Crafts. At that time Park and Bischoff were painting in figurative idioms, a treatment of the human figure which has been called lyrical abstraction and which influenced Diebenkorn's art.

Bath, painted in 1960, shows a thorough synthesis of Matisse, Hopper, and Abstract Expressionist handling of paint. A nude woman steps out of her bath. She gazes through a doorway much like a Hopper figure. This rich blue open space is flanked by white walls and panels of black and white tiles to form the room. The checkerboard pattern is at once floor and wainscoting. The result is a shallow pictorial space reminiscent of Matisse. Thinner washes of white applied over a darker color emphasize the use of strokes to form the wall. The figure is similarly modeled, although in reverse. Darker washes are applied over heavy pink impasto to define the woman's body. This exposure of process and heavy brushwork is an Abstract Expressionist trait. The geometric patterns, seductive colors, and lush thick paint engage and delight the viewer to the point of making him forget the subject—a figure alone in a pensive and vulnerable moment.

H.B.

Buck, Robert T., Jr., and Linda L. Cathcart, Gerald Nordland, Maurice Tuchman. *Richard Diebenkorn: Paintings and Drawings, 1943-1976.* Buffalo, N.Y.: Albright-Knox Art Gallery, 1976.

Painting and Sculpture in California: the modern era. San Francisco: Museum of Modern Art, 1977.

Russell, John. *Richard Diebenkorn; The Ocean Park Series: Recent Work.* London: Marlborough Fine Art, Ltd., 1971.

MORRIS GRAVES (b. 1910)

12. GOTHIC BIRD, 1954

Gouache on paper
42 1/2 x 16 (108.0 x 40.6)
Signed lower right: *M. Graves*
Williams College Museum of Art

Born in Oregon in 1910, Morris Graves is a Pacific Northwest artist who is largely self-taught. On a 1928 visit to the Orient Graves discovered Zen Buddhism, which quickly became an important part of his life and has remained a constant source of inspiration. Graves feels he is continually striving to free himself from some inner bondage; he projects this self-image in pictures of birds trapped in masses of white light or blinded and shut off from normal existence.

For Graves, the importance of the Orient and Buddhism was enhanced by the influence of Mark Tobey, a Pacific Northwest artist who had studied with the Chinese painter Teng Kwei in Shanghai. By 1934 Tobey had evolved a system of "white writing" to create his pictures of snakes and birds. Graves adopted the "white writing" calligraphy and executed several pictures showing birds caught in webs of white light. These works were shown in Graves' first one-man show at the Seattle Art Museum in 1936; later they were brought to New York to be exhibited at the Museum of Modern Art in *Americans 1942.*

Gothic Bird dates from 1954, a period when Graves was already established as an artist. The creature's body is formed with short, sketchy brushstrokes culminating in a detailed rendering of the head. The colors are earth colors, soft blacks and browns with white for the feathers on the body and fur on the head. Both the artistic technique, similar to the monochrome ink paintings of Ch'an or Zen, and the coloring, common in many Eastern works, stem from the Orient. The composition of a lone figure placed against an empty background is also based on Eastern precedents. In accordance with Zen teachings, Graves uses a blank vista and background to allow the mind to lose itself in the mystical voids. This work may have been inspired by Chinese bronze tomb sculptures which Graves first saw while studying at the Honolulu Academy of Art

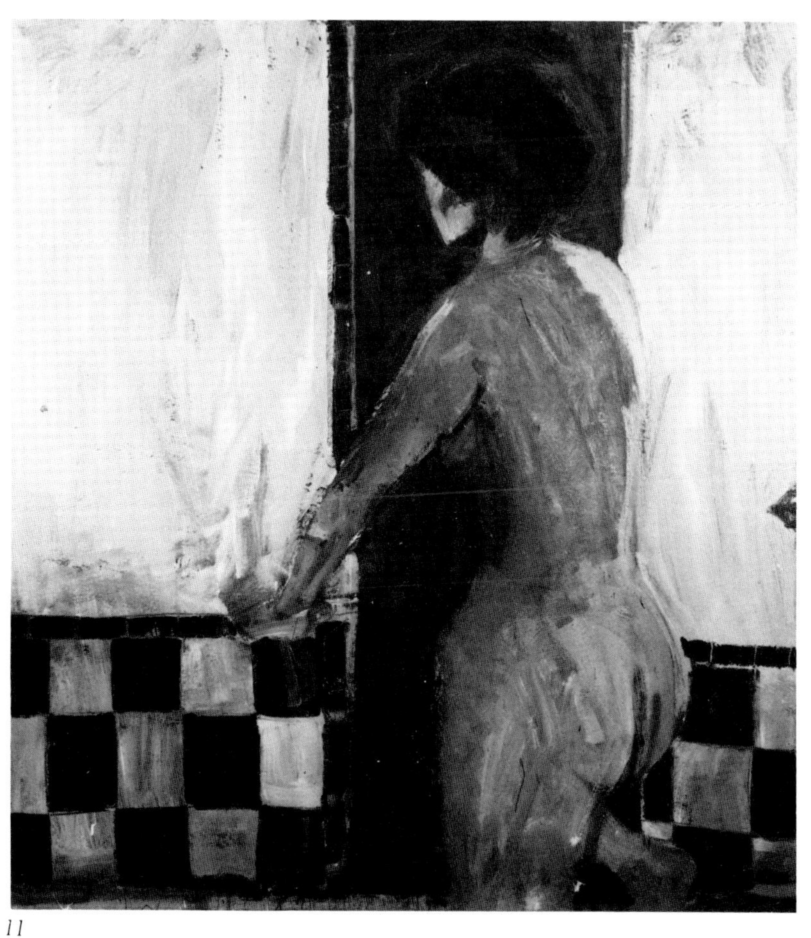
11

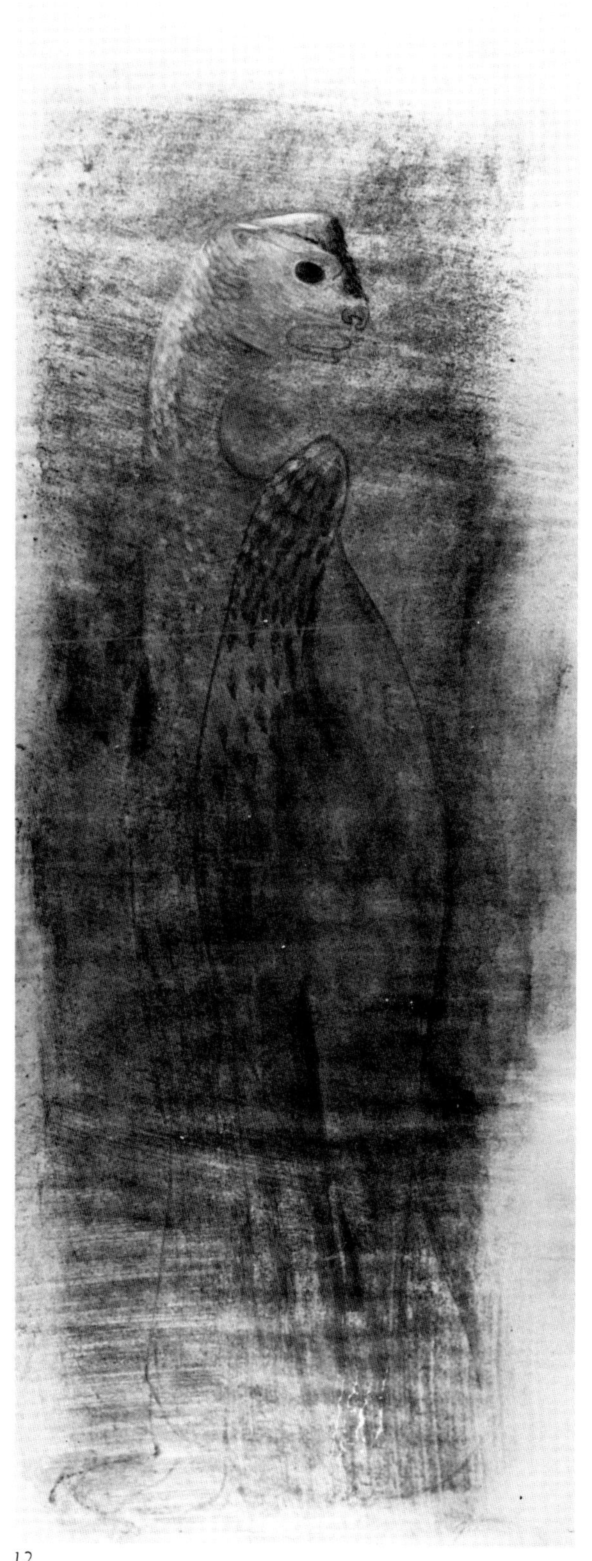
12

in 1947. These ritual bronzes from the Shang and Chou dynasties were symbolic pieces made up of conceptual animal and bird parts. *Gothic Bird* is not really a bird, but rather a fantastic gargoyle-like creature that is a combination rodent with an otter's head and bird with a hawk's body. The Chinese tomb sculptures stood guard over the deceased. Graves' *Gothic Bird* is perhaps meant to symbolize a keeper or custodian over man's psyche (Cohen, p. 16).

M.S.

Cohen, G. M. "Bird Paintings of Morris Graves." *College Art Journal*, vol. 18, no. 1, February 1958, pp. 2–19.
Smith, Vic. "Morris Graves," *Artform*, vol. 1 no. 11, May 1963, pp. 30–31.
Valentiner, W. R. "Morris Graves," *Art Quarterly*, Vol. 7, 1944, pp. 250–56.

MARSDEN HARTLEY (?) (1877–1943)

13. MUSHROOMS, 1940

Oil on board
19 ¾ x 23 ¾ (50.2 x 60.3)
Signed and dated lower left: *Marsden Hartley 19*
Williams College Museum of Art

The explorative vigor of Marsden Hartley's work made it a dominant force in the development of American abstract painting. His art, like his life, was marked by dramatic shifts in style and direction. Hartley first came to notice in 1909 when a selection of his "dark landscapes"—reminiscent of Ryder—were exhibited at Alfred Stieglitz's "291" New York gallery. Stieglitz, who became Hartley's chief sponsor, superintended his conversion to modernism, introducing him to the then radical work of Cézanne, Matisse and Picasso. In Germany he met Kandinsky and other artists of "der Blaue Reiter," whose belief in the supremacy of personal expression and the spirituality of abstract imagery encouraged Hartley's own investigations into pure abstraction. The culmination of these early experiments was a spectacular series of "German officer portraits" (1914–15), constructed from the patterns and forms of military insignia. Unfortunately, the exhilarating momentum of his German paintings could not be sustained after his return home in 1915. Received in New York with indifference, even hostility, Hartley's work faltered. His confidence broken, he retreated to the security of a more traditional, representational art, producing landscapes and still lifes in a confusion of borrowed styles. Only late in life, after nearly two aimless decades, did Hartley recover the strength and clarity of his true voice. His late paintings, while still "representational," project an immediate and overwhelming abstract presence. Their power rests in their capacity to communicate profoundly and simultaneously with both the conscious and subconscious of the viewer.

Painted in 1940, *Mushrooms* exemplifies Hartley's ability to bind simple, direct forms and colors into cohesive, powerful relationships. The objects, reduced to a few softly modeled shapes, are seen from above, thus tending to collapse the pictorial space. Furthermore, the spiraling tension of the composition exerts a subtle outward pressure on the viewer's own space. The overall texture of crisp, jaunty brushstrokes emphasizes the surface, while at the same time asserting the intensity and immediacy of the artist's experience.

Recent extensive cleaning and repair of this painting have raised some questions regarding its authenticity that have not been fully answered. Until they are, it seems prudent to assign this work to Hartley with a question mark, until all of the evidence is gathered and experts in the field render their opinions.

J.C.

Hartley, Marsden. "Art and the Personal Life." *Creative Art*, June 1928, pp. 31–37.
Haskell, Barbara. *Marsden Hartley*. New York: Whitney Museum of American Art, 1980.
Levin, Gail. "Marsden Hartley and the European Avant-Garde." *Arts Magazine*, vol. 54, September 1979, pp. 158–163.

ROBERT HENRI (1865–1929)

14. BLACKWELL'S ISLAND, EAST RIVER, 1900

Oil on canvas
20 x 24 ¼ (51.0 x 61.6)
Signed lower left: *Robert Henri*
Whitney Museum of American Art

Born in Cincinnati in 1864, Robert Henri enrolled in the Pennsylvania Academy of the Fine Arts in 1886 and studied there under Thomas Anshutz. In 1888 he went to Paris and enrolled in the Académie Julian, where he received a thorough training in the traditional academic manner. However, he soon came to regard the methods and results of academism as too staid for his tastes and he was drawn to more innovative styles, including Impressionism. When he returned to Philadelphia in 1891 he was painting in a style which reflected this new interest.

In 1895 Henri went back to Paris and in the following years several of his works were shown in the

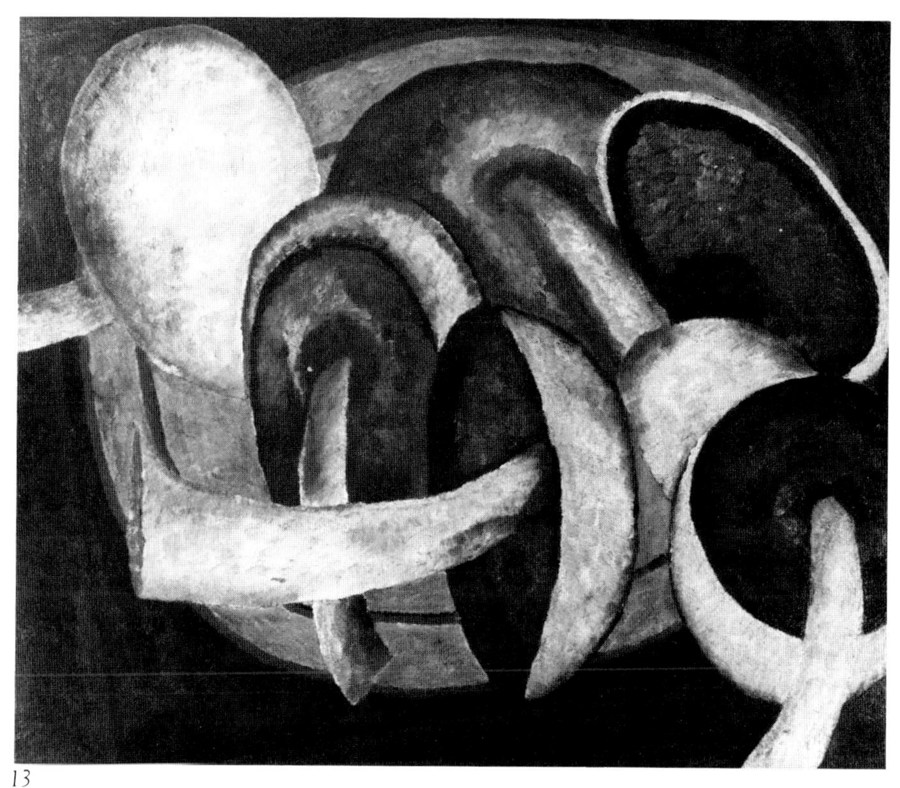

13

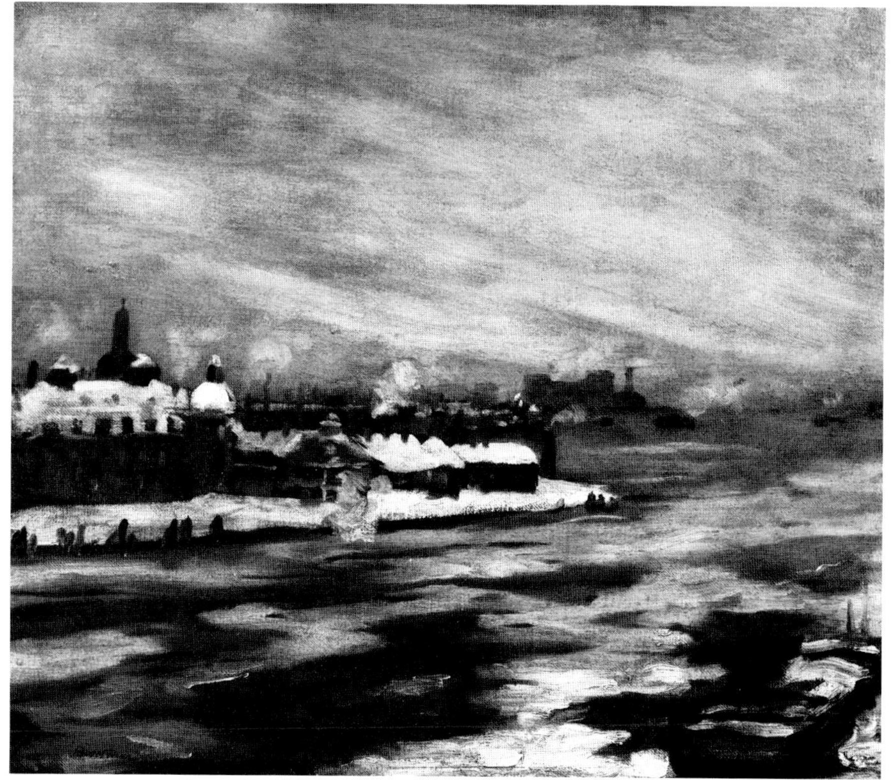

14

French Salons. He had long admired Spanish and Dutch painting, in particular that of Velazquez and Hals, and the free brushwork and low-keyed color of these works suggest their influence as well as that of Manet, whose paintings Henri had studied in Paris.

Henri's reputation was secured by his Salon successes. He doubtless could have remained in Paris and pursued a fruitful career there, but in 1900 he resolved to return to America. His dealer, William Macbeth, urged him to paint works which sensitively portrayed the ever-changing moods of the thriving city.

Blackwell's Island, East River belongs to this group. In 1900 Henri and his wife took a house overlooking the East River which provided excellent views of the busy waterfront. Fascinated by the dark forms of warehouses and wharves and by the constant traffic of ships and small boats, Henri frequently painted views of the river. The present work shows a scene in the cold of winter. The gray, streaked sky overhead is echoed by the ice-and-snow-jammed river. On the shore the white masses of snow and steam contrast vividly with the somber buildings and piers. Detail has been ignored in favor of a spontaneous and fluid handling. Certain areas are richly built up in pigment; Henri had an intuitive grasp of the tactile qualities of paint, and such passages are a hallmark of his style. Color, in keeping with the season and like his earlier Parisian works, is subdued. A few carefully placed touches of red—on the boat's bow, stern, and stack and on the smokestacks of the buildings on shore—enliven the scene. The result is a painting in which Henri's distinctive technique is harmoniously blended with his honest approach to factual appearance.

F.W.K.

Geske, Norman A. *Robert Henri*, Catalogue of an exhibition held in observance of the centennial of the artist's birth, Sheldon Memorial Art Gallery. University of Nebraska, Lincoln, 1965.

Goodman, Helen. "Robert Henri, Teacher." *Arts Magazine*, vol. 53, no. 1, September 1978, pp. 158-60.

Homer, William Innes. *Robert Henri and His Circle*. Ithaca: Cornell University Press, 1969.

EDWARD HOPPER (1882–1967)

15. RANCH HOUSE, SANTA FE, 1925

Watercolor over graphite on paper
13 3/4 x 19 3/4 (34.9 x 50.2)
Signed and dated lower right: *Edward Hopper 1925*
Williams College Museum of Art

16. MORNING IN A CITY, 1944

Oil on canvas
44 1/8 x 60 1/4 (112.1 x 152.4)
Signed lower right: *Edward Hopper*
Williams College Museum of Art

Edward Hopper, born in 1882, began his artistic career as a commercial artist. In 1900 he began studies at the New York School of Art under Robert Henri, and spent the next ten years traveling intermittently to Europe in order to study and paint firsthand. Hopper sold his first painting at the famous Armory Show in 1913 and thereafter continued to lead several artistic lives—as a commercial illustrator, an art student in New York, and an active artist abroad. He worked especially hard at the last, and by 1924 he had mounted successful exhibitions in New York of his French work, which included paintings and watercolors. The following year Hopper married Josephine Nivison, who was to be his lifelong companion and champion of his art, and the two set out on their first trip west, winding up in Santa Fe, New Mexico.

Ranch House, Santa Fe was executed on that trip. The watercolor medium was essentially all but abandoned by Hopper later in life, but at this stage of his career he used it often and to great effect. The adobe building is shown in a sunlit setting devoid of people, with an austere, sharp clarity that becomes Hopper's trademark. Washes are laid on delicately to preserve the white luminosity of the paper; dark flashes of Prussian blue intensify the shadows. Hopper skillfully and quickly renders the hot, dry ambience of the southwestern desert.

By 1933 Hopper's reputation was so well established that the Museum of Modern Art felt compelled to give him a retrospective. The artist spent the following two decades traveling throughout North America, especially the Southwest and Mexico, with the same enthusiasm that he had earlier shown for Europe. By the time Hopper painted *Morning in a City*, his style was fully formed and his themes totally conceived. Lone figures in an urban setting became for the artist a way of treating the changes of wartime society. The nude woman in the unadorned, sunlit room is depicted in the mundane art of dressing. But there is more there: she gazes absently out the open window, as vulnerable and lonely in her thoughts as in her physical being. The vista through the window offers no relief; rather, more bleakness and solitude. Hopper's smoothly painted and ordered spaces reinforce the feeling of drabness and spiritual emptiness in city life that Thomas Wolfe described in his novels of the period. His vision would always remain so.

R.S.

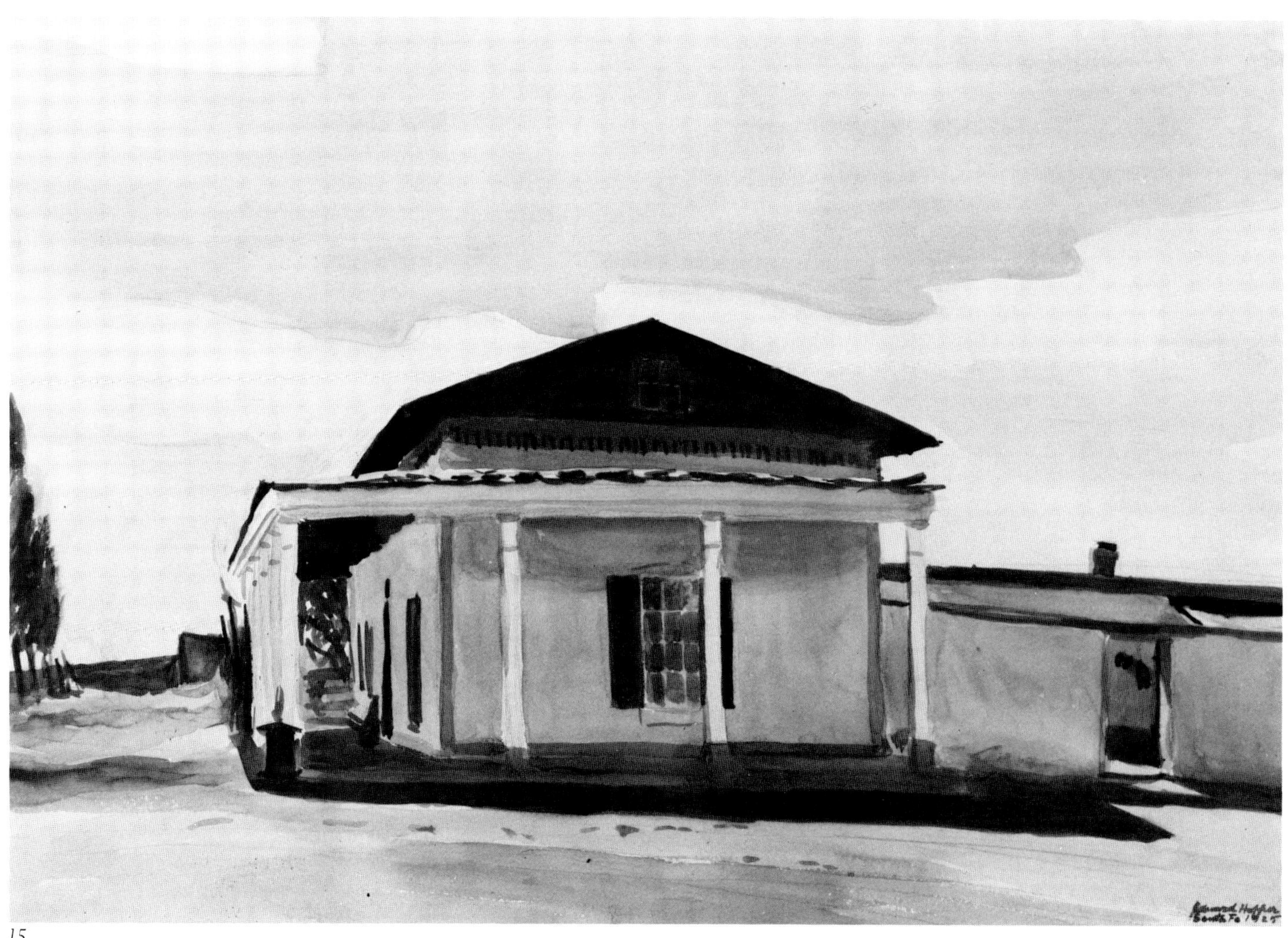

15

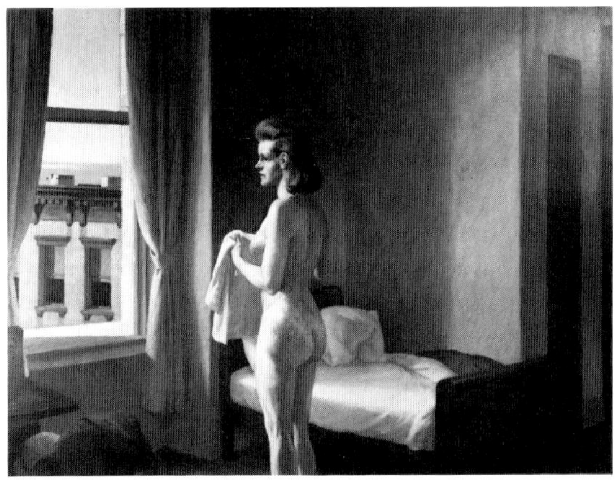

16

Barr, Alfred H., Jr., and Charles Burchfield. *Edward Hopper Retrospective*. New York: Museum of Modern Art, 1933.

Goodrich, Lloyd. *Edward Hopper*. New York: Harry N. Abrams, 1978.

Goodrich, Lloyd. *Edward Hopper*. New York: Whitney Museum of American Art, 1964.

Lanes, Jerrold. "Edward Hopper." *Artforum*, vol. 7, October 1968, pp. 44–49.

ROBERT INDIANA (b. 1928)

17. THE AMERICAN WAY: EAT #3, 1964

Conte crayon on paper (stencil rubbing)
30 1/8 x 22 1/16 (76.5 x 56.0)
Signed and dated lower right: *Robert Indiana '64*
Williams College Museum of Art

The artist was born Robert Clark in New Castle, Indiana in 1928. He settled in New York in 1954 and rented a loft in a group of derelict warehouses on Coenties Slip on the East River in lower Manhattan. On the slip, Indiana met other artists, notably Ellsworth Kelly, and became aware of the signs and words around him, words that were to influence the rest of his career as a Pop artist.

In 1961 Robert Indiana declared himself "an American painter of signs" (Penn. Cat. 1968, p. 9), and these two ideas—the idea of "signs," and that of "American-ness"—are inherent in his work. The signs evolve from commercial pieces like diner signs and stop signs, and are used as symbols to comment on the advertising- and publicity-oriented state of our existence. Both ideas are present in *The American Way: Eat #3*, which was executed as part of a series entitled "The American Dream"—a series inspired both by Indiana's own experiences and by Edward Albee's play of the same name. *Eat #3* (1964) represents one of the series' early "dreams," which the artist says were "cynical, I was really being very critical of certain aspects of the American experience" (University of Texas interview, Sept. 1977).

This work is a rubbing done from a stencil similar in form to the stencil for the American Hay Company which, according to Indiana, inspired him toward Pop art. The word "Eat" is made into a sort of icon in this carefully rubbed drawing. The stencil was not randomly shaded over; rather, each crayon line is distinctly visible and separate. Gradations in color and tone are achieved through a concentration of straight bold lines. The lines which radiate out from the central Eat sign lead the eye in a circular pattern and emphasize the shape.

M.S.

Robert Indiana. Austin: University of Texas Art Museum, 1977.

Robert Indiana. Introduction by John McCoubrey. Philadelphia: University of Pennsylvania, Institute of Contemporary Art, 1968.

Raynor, Vivien. "The Man who Invented Love." *Art News*, vol. 72, February 1973, pp. 58–62.

Swenson, G. R. "The New American Sign Painters." *Art News*, vol. 61, September 1962, pp. 44–47.

DONG KINGMAN (b. 1911)

18. SIGNAL WATCHER, c. 1952

Watercolor on paper
21 1/8 x 29 1/8 (53.7 x 74)
Signed lower right: *Dong Kingman*
Williams College Museum of Art

Dong Kingman was born in the Chinese section of Oakland, California, in 1911. When he was five, his family moved to Hong Kong, where his father established a successful department store. Impressed by his son's drawing ability, Kingman's father enrolled him in the Lingnan Academy; there the young art student soon attracted the attention of a painting teacher who had been educated in Paris and was, like Kingman, a product of East and West. As a result, his instruction involved a blending of the oriental *Hsieh-Yi* ("to draw from a conception") and the western *Hsieh-Cheng* ("to draw reality"), and Dong Kingman's art has always exemplified the brilliant interaction of these two fundamental approaches.

Returning to America at the age of eighteen, Kingman worked at a series of odd jobs to support his painting until he was given steady employment as an artist for the Works Progress Administration in 1936. During World War II he served with distinction in the OSS; upon his discharge he moved to New York, where he still lives today. It was in this

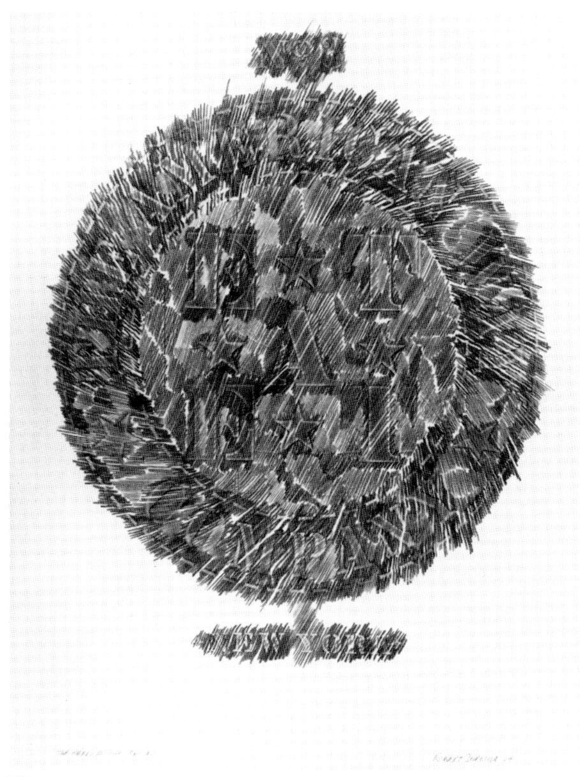
17

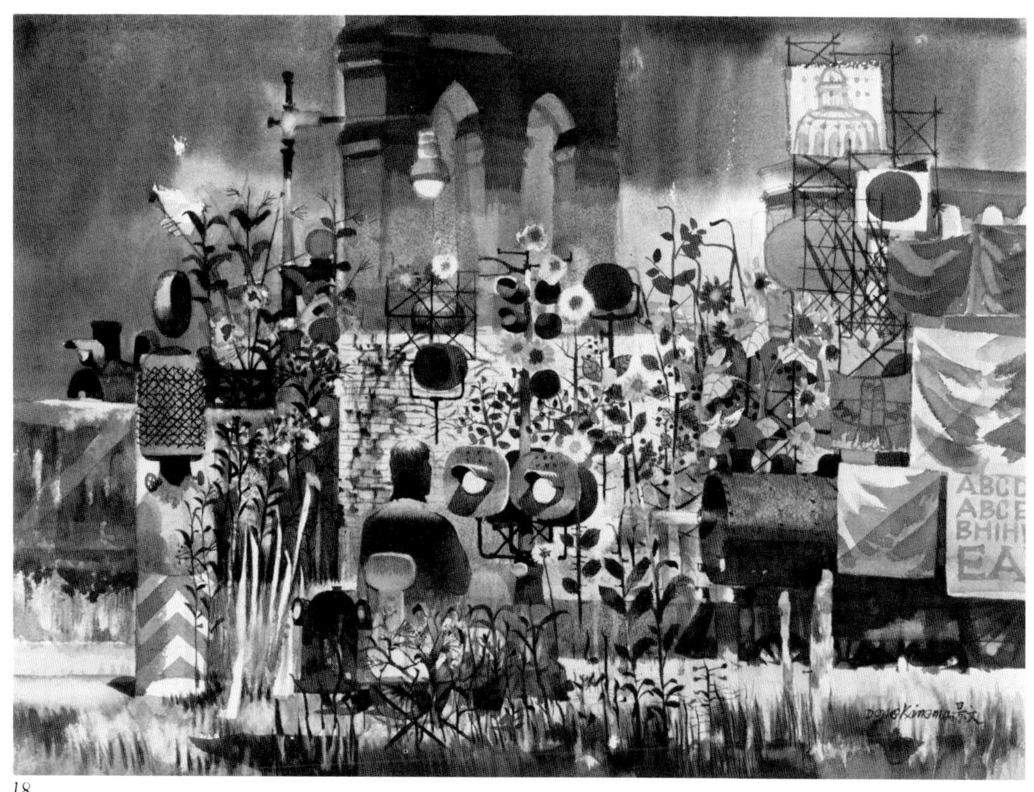
18

period that he developed the artistic style that made him famous. *Signal Watcher*, the work in this exhibition, was painted around 1952 at the height of the artist's powers, and affords easy access to the fundamental characteristics of his art.

Dong Kingman is a fluid and very complex watercolorist. *Signal Watcher* is a tapestry of delicate washes, overlays, and deft strokes in varied color. As always, Kingman's imagery is provocative, akin to the Surrealist employment of realistic elements juxtaposed in such a way as to afford improbable but intriguing relationships. A lone figure sits in a nondescript chair in an overgrown field populated by a gas pump, a moving locomotive, railroad and street signals, studio lights, and scaffolding with brightly colored banners. Above all this, a single stanchion from the Brooklyn Bridge dissolves into the liquid sky. It is an incongruous environment of variety, contrast, and strangeness; at the same time, its tightly controlled composition and carefully orchestrated color give it a sense of order and continuity. *Signal Watcher* embodies the best qualities of an artist fascinated by the absurdity and richness of New York City life. It is a perfect synthesis, as is all his best work, of *Hsieh-Yi* and *Hsieh-Cheng*.

R.S.

Gruskin, Alan. *Dong Kingman*. New York: Thomas Y. Crowell, 1958.

Letter from the artist, August 22, 1979.

JACK LEVINE (b. 1915)

19. THE JUDGE, 1953

Oil on canvas
42 x 48 (106.7 x 122.0)
Signed lower right: *J. Levine*
Williams College Museum of Art

"I am primarily concerned with the condition of man," Jack Levine has said. His paintings are viewed as satirical comments on modern society done by an artist who came to maturity during the Great Depression. The son of immigrant parents, Levine grew up in Boston's South End, which was a teeming theater of human comedy and tragedy. He studied with Denman W. Ross at Harvard and was trained in a traditional approach to figure painting which included assiduous absorption of the Old Masters. In the late 1930s, while working for the WPA art projects, Levine became moderately famous for his controversial paintings depicting the "minions of the law" who lived and worked within modern American society; figures of crooked contractors, racketeers, policemen, politicians and judges belied the rich colors and textures of his painted surfaces. It was in this period that Levine developed his "astigmatic" technique of breaking solid objects into mirrored faces or reflections, a technique that he felt better expressed his painterly emotions.

After serving in World War II Levine settled in New York to paint and exhibit regularly. Receipt of a Guggenheim Fellowship in 1947 enabled him to study in Europe for a year, and he returned to paint his subjects with a greater degree of formal understanding, as evidenced in *The Judge*. The work was painted in 1953, the same year as his most famous painting, *Gangster's Funeral*. By this time Levine had altered his social satire to encompass a broader intent: the judge depicted here, rather than being portrayed as either good or evil, simply is shown in the act of deliberation—an effect strengthened by the nebulous void to his left. The painting represents Levine's mature style; planes are broken up in a softly expressionistic way, creating an ambience rather than an impression. A work like *The Judge* reveals a mature artist, one who is no longer simply polemic but is instead thoughtfully analytic of the human condition.

R.S.

Getlein, Frank. *Jack Levine*. New York: Harry N. Abrams, Inc., 1966.

Levine, Jack. "Man is the Center." *Reality: A Journal of Artists' Opinions*, vol. 1, Spring 1953, pp. 5-6.

STANTON MacDONALD-WRIGHT (1890–1973)

20. STILL LIFE SYNCHROMY #3, 1928

Oil on canvas
19 1/4 x 24 1/4 (48.9 x 61.6)
Signed and dated on verso: *S. MacDonald-Wright 1928*
Williams College Museum of Art

It was in Paris in late 1910 or early 1911 that Stanton MacDonald-Wright met Morgan Russell and founded the Synchromist movement, meaning, literally, "with color." In 1913 Wright explained that "Form to me is color. When I conceive a composition of form my imagination creates an organization of color that corresponds to it" (Scott, p.11). Wright and Russell attempted to create form in space through the optically advancing and receding nature of color. Differences in values and the luminosity of colors aided their illusion of depth.

Still Life Synchromy #3 was executed in 1928, by which date Wright had moved away from painting non-objective works. Through the twenties, objects

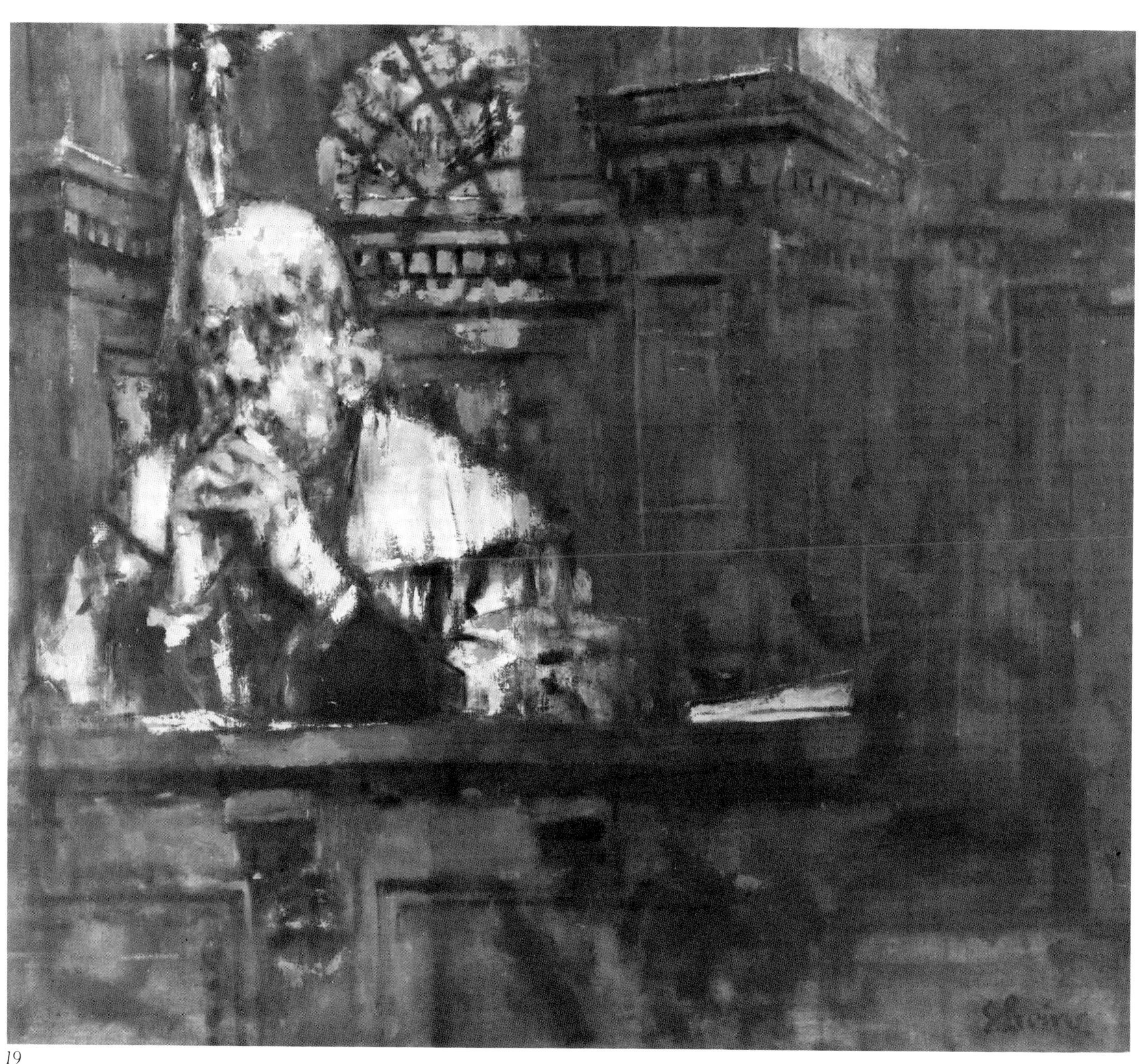

19

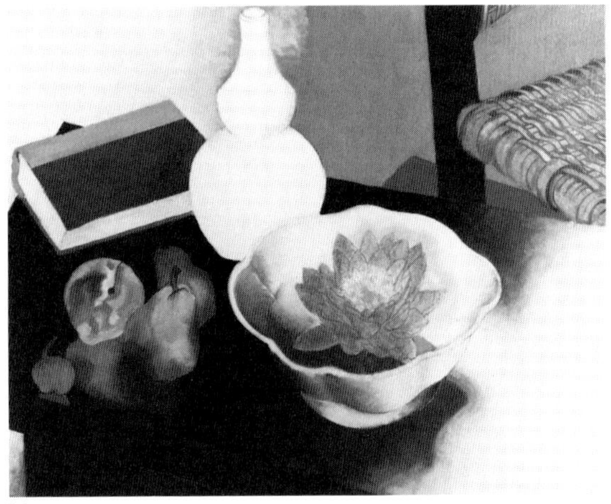
20

and figures became increasingly more important in his compositions. This painting belongs to Wright's long experimental period when he varied his technique in search of the right form to express himself. Wright mainly painted still lifes in this manner in 1927 and 1928, but some are dated as late as 1931. By 1925 Wright's color is still largely pure but it is no longer in spectral suites. The color adheres more to the local color of the object depicted, and the inner parts of defined areas are often a solid color. The black table, white vase and violet book exemplify this in *Still Life Synchromy #3*. However, Wright then paints the fruit and bowl in a Cézannesque manner, with mixed watery translucent colors. Wright greatly admired Cézanne and painted earlier still lifes in a style reminiscent of his works. The juxtaposition of the translucent and solid colors is one of the striking and experimental elements in this work, as Wright rarely uses color in the same way in other paintings.

The painting shows influences from other sources as well, and it can be seen as a synthesis of styles that interested and influenced Wright at the time. The subject matter, as well as the flattened representation of the objects, shows an affinity to the still lifes of painters like Georges Braque in the same period. Likewise, the manner in which the subject is cropped by the edges of the painting is a convention that MacDonald-Wright adapted from his study of Chinese art forms.

L.J.

Levin, Gail. *Synchromism and American Color Abstraction 1910–1925*. New York: George Braziller, Inc., and the Whitney Museum of American Art, 1978.

Scott, David W. *Stanton MacDonald-Wright*. Washington: National Collection of Fine Arts, 1967.

Walker, John Alan. "Interview: Stanton MacDonald-Wright." January-February 1974, pp 59–65.

LOREN MacIVER (b. 1909)

21. PARIS NIGHT MEANDERS, 1959

Oil on canvas
42 x 57 (106.7 x 144.8)
Signed lower left: *MacIver*
Whitney Museum of American Art

Throughout her career, Loren MacIver has painted visions of a private world of fantasy and wonder. "It sometimes seems as if she deliberately sought to preserve a child-like innocence in both her paintings and her relations with the world" (Baur, p. 7). In the *Fourteen Americans* catalogue of the Museum of Modern Art she explains succinctly her intent as an artist: "Quite simple things can lead to discovery. This is what I would like to do with painting: starting with simple things, to lead the eye by various manipulations of colors, objects and tensions toward a transformation and a reward."

MacIver gained full artistic maturity at the beginning of the forties. As her ability to create more complex abstract compositions grew, her poetic vision expanded to include subjects of greater dimension. The city became a principal theme of her work. She made her first voyage to Europe in 1948, returning the following year to paint furiously, producing works of greater richness and size.

Paris Night Meanders, painted in 1959, follows this line of development. MacIver says that it is about "leisurely strolls in Paris at night, illuminated by pietons, those metal discs (used at) street crossings" (from a letter to the author, 1978). Her symbols have become even more ephemeral; three key holes, a crescent moon, a wine decanter, a loaf of bread, ivy and, to the far left, an oval shape covered with sequins of black and white paint are suspended in an atmosphere of delicate gray tonalities. This atmosphere is composed of the textures of cobblestones, stone walls, and clouds through which filters the light of the crescent moon. Over the gray tonalities are strokes of maroon, dark blue, yellow and neon green; the technique of laying pale transparent hues over a dark ground is one which MacIver developed during the fifties.

Paris Night Meanders is a dreamlike vision; one imagines the small hidden alleyways of Paris known only to those who have a sense for such illusive spaces. The work is exquisitely painted, full of sen-

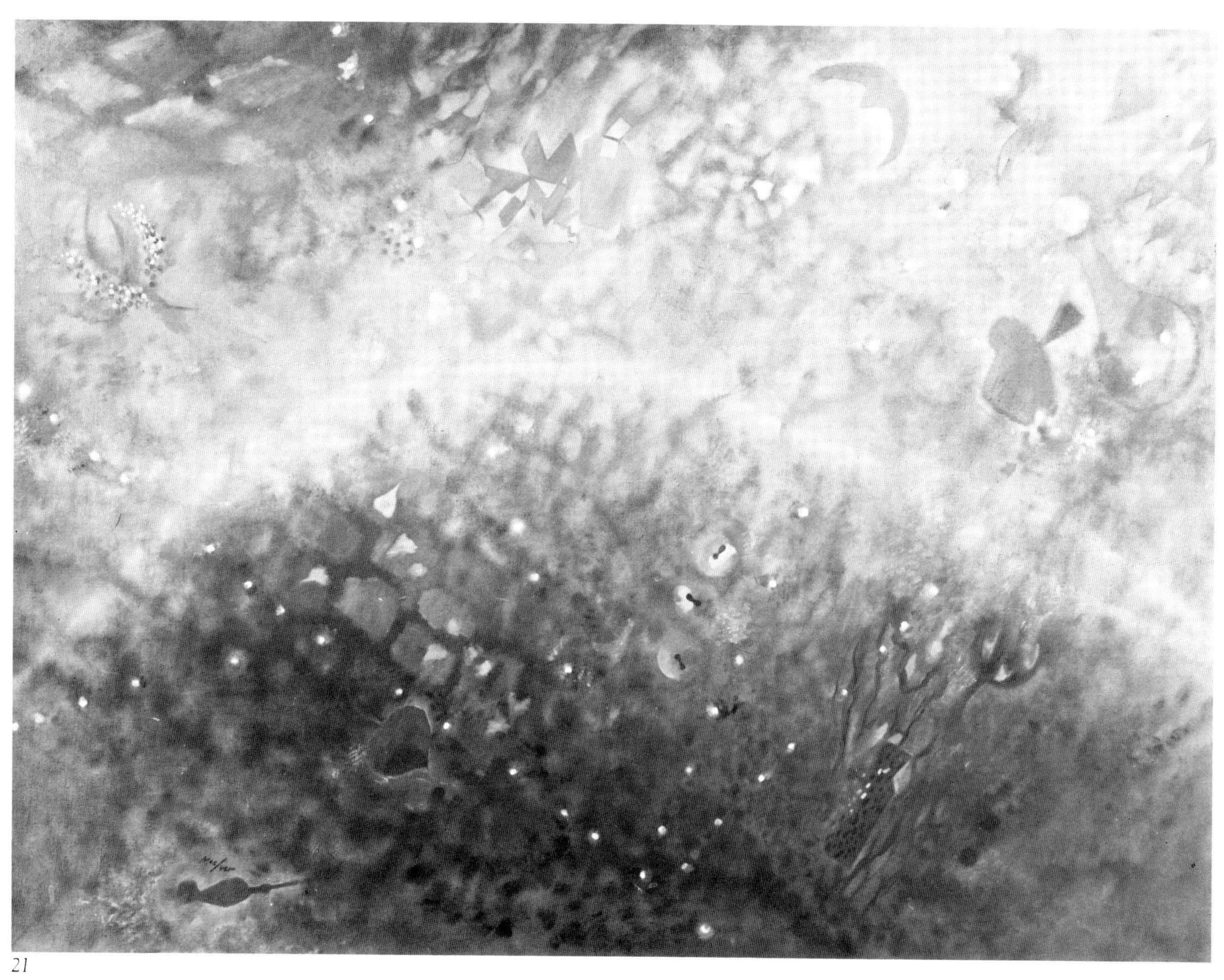

21

sitive detail. The layered texture of the gray background seems to combine several views in an image. MacIver has often used this technique to convey the richness of her poetic vision.

A.S.

Baur, John I. H. *MacIver/Pereira*. New York: Whitney Museum of American Art, 1953.

Miller, Dorothy. *14 Americans*. New York: Museum of Modern Art, 1946.

Interview with the artist, November 1978.

JOHN MARIN (1870–1953)

22. STONINGTON, MAINE, 1919

Watercolor on paper
19 ½ x 16 ½ (49.5 x 41.9)
Signed and dated lower right: *Marin 19*
Williams College Museum of Art

In 1905 John Marin sailed for Paris to pursue his painting career. While in Europe, he was greatly influenced by Whistler, both in his development of an etching style and in his watercolors and paintings. Around 1908, however, the Post-Impressionism of Bonnard and Signac seems to have become an influence as well. Present in most of Marin's works of this period is a tendency to reduce many of the forms to a simplified motif, which would be an important element of his future style.

Marin returned permanently to the United States in 1911 and for the next several years began to develop a more abstract and dynamic vocabulary. After a trip to Maine in 1914 he became more passionately involved with nature than ever before, and the New England landscape and coastline became the major subject of his work for the rest of his career.

Stonington, Maine was executed in 1919, when Marin was still experimenting with his vocabulary, yet was approaching maturity in his ability to communicate his impressions. Rather than being concerned with a broad view of nature, Marin concentrates on a single subject, a boat, and brings the viewer almost on top of it, with the boat crowding out of the front of the picture plane. Form has been abstracted to a marked degree, with the various elements of the schooner suggested through linear and wavy strokes. Bits of rigging, the masts and the bow are all disconnected fragments, left to the viewer to re-associate. Color, too, is more abstract and suggestive than representational, and is fairly broad in palette, although Marin's favorite blue/gray scheme is still dominant. A patch of green behind the boat gives a suggestion of land; washes of salmon and pale yellow in the sky indicate sunlight. A few intense strokes of bright blue and yellow further suggest the glint of rays and water.

The summer of 1919 was Marin's first in Stonington, a far livelier spot than his previous Maine locations. A sense of the movement of this harbor is communicated in the watercolor through the single form of the boat. The geometric patterns of the mast and rigging, with their strong verticals and diagonals, lend an impression of counteractive motion, while the two bow forms suggest up-and-down movement.

L.C.

Curry, Larry. *John Marin: 1870–1953*. Los Angeles: Los Angeles County Museum of Art, 1970.

Norman, Dorothy. *John Marin: Selected Writings*. New York: Pelligrini and Cudahy, 1949.

Reich, Sheldon. *John Marin: A Stylistic Analysis and Catalogue Raisonné*. Tucson: University of Arizona Press, 1970.

ALICE TRUMBULL MASON (1904–1971)

23. SURFACE WINDS (SUSPENSION POINTS), 1959

Oil on canvas
30 x 36 ⅛ (76.2 x 91.8)
Signed and dated lower right corner: *A.T.M. 1959*
Whitney Museum of American Art

Alice Trumbull Mason was born into a well-to-do New England family that included the famous Revolutionary War painter John Trumbull among its ancestors. From 1924 to 1928 Mason executed paintings in a Manet-like style under Charles Hawthorne at the National Academy of Design in New York. The opening of the Museum of Modern Art in 1928 was of great significance for the abstract direction of her art, as were her studies with Arshile Gorky at the Grand Central Galleries and a trip she made in 1929–30 to Greece and southern Italy in order to study Byzantine mosaics.

Mason's paintings of the 1930s and early 1940s reveal a debt to Gorky and Miró, in their use of biomorphic shapes which are cut through with long, sharp lines that create geometric areas. In the mid-1940s Mason's paintings began to show the influence of Mondrian, who had arrived in New York in 1940, and she joined the American Abstract Artists in 1941. She subsequently created tightly-knit yet less crowded geometric compositions in both her paintings and in soft-ground etchings and aquatints, which she first practiced in *Atelier 17* between 1944 and 1947.

Painted toward the end of Mason's career, *Surface*

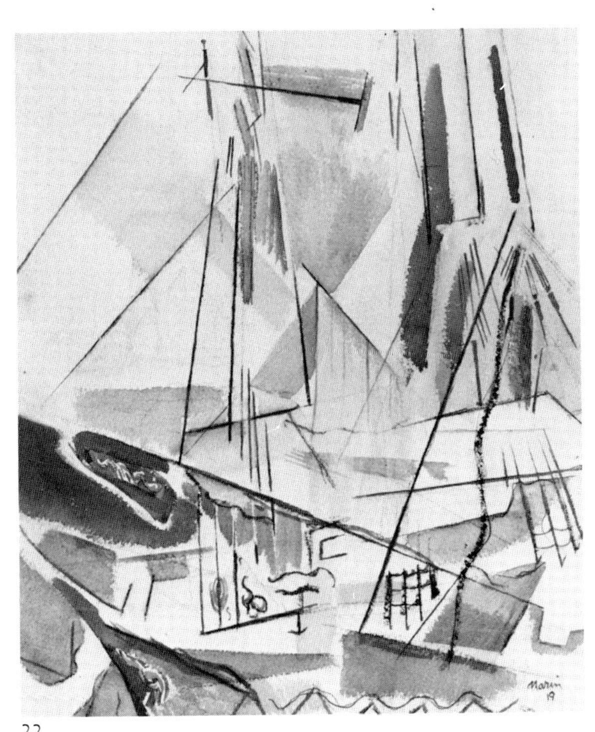

22

23

Winds, like all of her paintings, communicates fine tuning and choreography, partially a result of the craftsmanship involved. Mason not only made many preparatory drawings for her works but also made her own paints; hence the extremely delicate shifts in hues among the warm oranges, yellows and reds of *Surface Winds*. This painting distinguishes itself from other late works in its tilting rhythm. Whereas there is a strong vertical-horizontal orientation in most of the paintings of the late 1950s and early 1960s, the thin trapezoids and parallelograms of *Surface Winds* tip towards and away from each other in a way that harks back to earlier paintings, but involves less dramatic shifts in scale.

L.G.

Archives of American Art. Alice Trumbull Mason papers. Reel N69/167.

Foote, Linda. "Alice Trumbull Mason." In *Women Artists: 1550–1950*, text by Ann Sutherland Harris and Linda Nochlin, pp. 327–28. New York: Los Angeles County Museum and Alfred A. Knopf, 1976.

Larsen, Susan Carol. "The American Abstract Artists Group: A History and Evaluation of its Impact upon American Art." Unpublished Ph.D dissertation, University of Michigan, 1975.

JAN MATULKA (1890–1972)

24. CUBIST STILL LIFE WITH GUITAR. Verso: SEATED FEMALE NUDE. n.d.

Conte crayon and pencil on paper
14 5/8 x 11 5/8 (37.5 x 29.8)
Signed in pencil, lower left: *Matulka*
Whitney Museum of American Art

Jan Matulka emigrated to the United States from what is now Czechoslovakia in 1907. In 1911 he began studying under George Willoughby Maynard at the National Academy of Design in New York. He had his first one-man show at the Whitney Studio Club in 1929, the year he began teaching at the Art Students League, where he remained until 1932.

Like the majority of Matulka's works, the Bloedel drawings are not dated. They can, however, be placed in the early 1920s, due to the similarity between *Cubist Still Life* and a 1923 drawing entitled *Abstract Forms* (illus., Yale University Art Gallery, 1950, p. 18). Both two-sided drawings of still lifes and female studies are executed in black Conte crayon; both still lifes involve a musical instrument split up into different parts which overlap with rays and swirls in a play of diagonal directions. While the breaking down of a musical instrument's classic shape is obviously a Cubist device, Matulka's incorporation of mysterious floating circles and crescent moons in the Bloedel drawing adds a cosmic dimension to the otherwise relatively derivative configuration with Picasso, Braque and Gris associations. The source for these elements is undoubtedly Kandinsky, whose paintings of the 1920s include crescents and circles along with other clear hard-edged geometric shapes. By combining such different sources as Kandinsky abstractions and Cubist still lifes, Matulka created an original modern still life.

Equally interesting is the female nude on the verso. The combination of simple flowing outline and careful cross-hatching reflects an austere classical effect possibly derived from André Derain.

Cubist Still Life is one of Matulka's most dynamic and inspired works. By successfully infusing Cubist-derived elements with a sense of dramatic motion, Matulka reflects a tendency among American artists of the 1920s, most notably Stuart Davis, to improvise on given Cubist formulas. Unlike Davis, Matulka did not pursue the personal vision of Cubist structure he achieved in the Bloedel drawing, but instead continued to work in a variety of styles, reflecting his simultaneous attraction to Realism and Abstraction.

L.G.

Avant-Garde Art: Painting and Sculpture in America 1910–1925. Wilmington: Delaware Art Museum, 1975.

Levin, Gail. *Synchromism and American Color Abstraction*. New York: Whitney Museum of American Art, 1978.

Sims, Patterson. *Jan Matulka*. New York: Whitney Museum of American Art, 1979.

ALFRED HENRY MAURER (1868–1932)

25. STILL LIFE, c. 1930

Oil on panel
13 5/8 x 30 1/2 (34.6 x 77.5)
Unsigned
Williams College Museum of Art

Alfred Maurer was born in New York City in 1868, the son of a commercial artist who had worked at one time as a lithographer for Currier and Ives. In 1897 Maurer departed for Paris, where he would remain with only brief visits home until 1914. Sometime around 1905 he abandoned a popular, acceptable style for a bolder, more experimental manner. He became acquainted with Alfred Stieglitz at about this time, probably through his friend Arthur Dove. In 1909 Maurer was given an exhibition at the "291" Gallery in New York, along with John Marin.

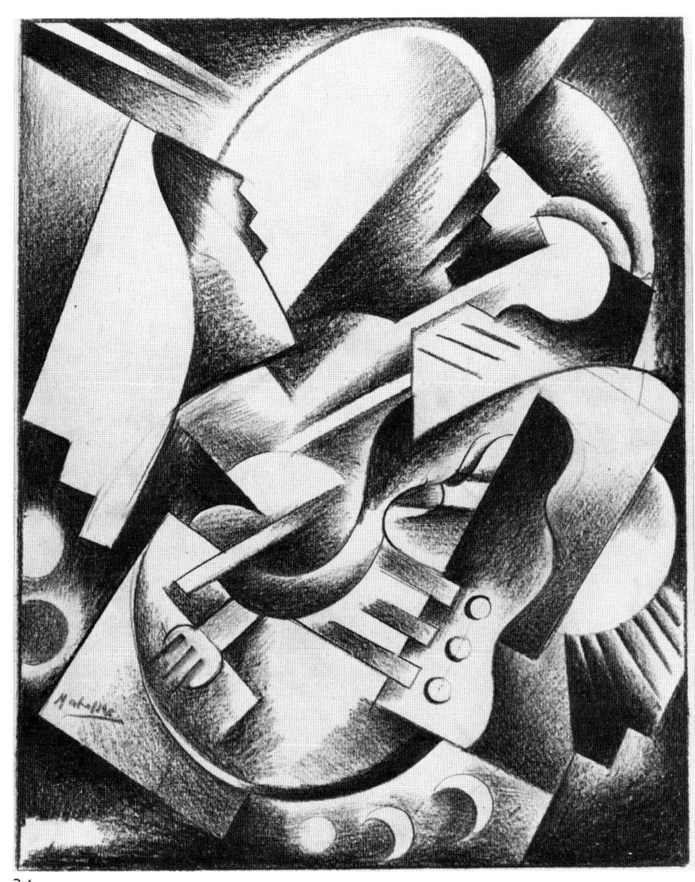

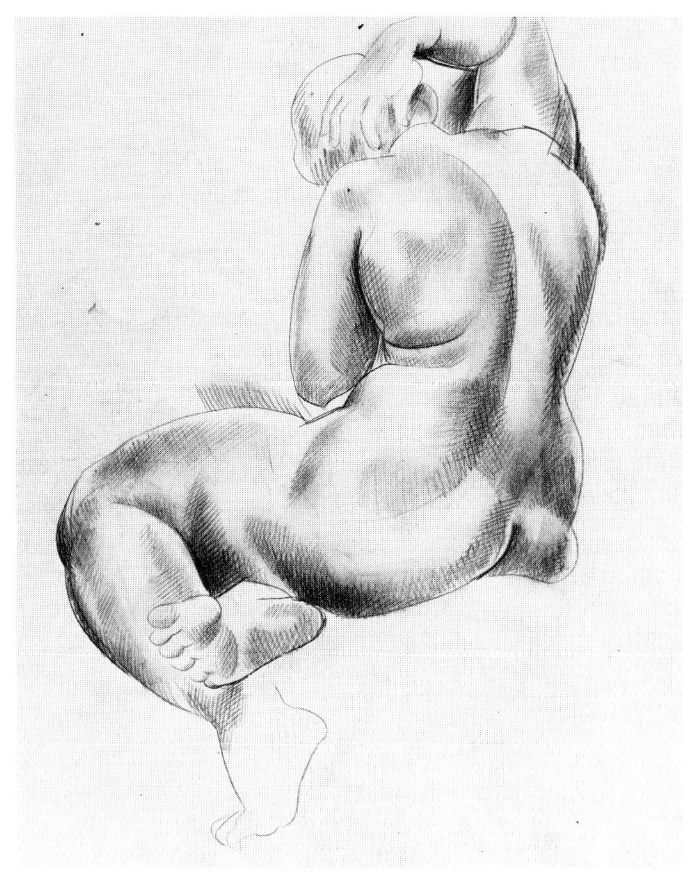

24

Maurer returned permanently to the United States with the outbreak of World War I. He soon became an active force in the Society of Independent Artists, and exhibited regularly; but during the late teens and early twenties there was very little recognition of his work. In 1924, however, a New York art dealer, Erhard Weyhe, bought out Maurer's entire studio and over the next years presented a number of one-man exhibitions.

Still Life was executed around 1930, only a few years before Maurer's death, and thus reflects some of the very last developments in his work. The surface of the painting is divided into geometric areas, many of which seem to be side by side, rather than planes on top of one another. The surfaces upon which the fruit is placed are two semi-rectangular areas, one black and one white. Behind these two planes are various divisions of different colors and textures, conveying an impression of different areas of the architectural setting. The colors are more subdued than Maurer's usual palette, with muddy yellows for the banana and lemon, a dull pink in the background, and various other rather earthy hues.

The rigid compartmentalization of the still life is indicative of a number of influences, the major one being Maurer's interest in the theory of "dynamic symmetry." Developed by Jay Hambidge, an artist of Maurer's acquaintance, this theory postulated a system of artistic design based upon sections of geometric forms placed in specific ratios to other forms. Design symmetry is seen also in the color scheme; the white shape and black shape seem almost complementary, particularly with the placement of the black walnut on the white surface and the white walnut on the black surface. The compartmentalization also seems to serve as a rigid attempt to order the elements, which convey an odd sense of motion—particularly the walnuts, which seem to be spilling across the surface. There is also a floating quality to the top surfaces, as if they will lose their stability and tip over at any minute.

In this still life we see many borrowings. The cream colored area with multi-colored strokes recalls the decorative interiors which Matisse executed during the twenties. The influence of Georges Braque's still lifes of the twenties is also strong, particularly in the use of decorative shadows for the objects, as well as their general arrangement. Maurer did not, however, merely assimilate forms without adding any of his own style or emotion; rather, he used Cubist elements as a point of departure for his own interests in formal organization.

L.C.

McCausland, Elizabeth. *A.H. Maurer*. New York: A.A. Wyn, 1951.

Reich, Sheldon. *A. H. Maurer*. Washington, D.C.: National Collection of Fine Arts, 1973.

Rosenfeld, Paul. "The Maurer Little Girl." *New Republic*, vol. 83, 30 November 1932, pp. 73–74.

GEORGE L. K. MORRIS (1905–1975)

26. PIVOT, 1964

Oil on canvas
48 x 36 (121.9 x 91.4)
Signed lower right: *Morris*
Whitney Museum of American Art

George L. K. Morris was born in 1905 in New York City to a wealthy family descended from one of the signers of the Declaration of Independence. After graduating from Yale, Morris studied at the Art Students League in New York from 1929 to 1930. He then traveled to Paris where he was introduced to Picasso, Braque, Brancusi and other renowned artists, and he remained there to study with Léger. Returning to the United States in 1932, Morris banded together with other artists who were interested in the post-Cubist experiments taking place in Paris.

In 1936 Morris, Alexander Calder, Charles Biederman, John Ferren, and Charles Shaw exhibited together at A. E. Gallatin's Museum of Living Art Gallery under the title of "Concretionists." In that same year, American Abstract Artists was formed, a diverse group of painters whose original purpose was simply to exhibit. By 1939, however, the organization had become more doctrinaire and no longer included artists who were not dedicated to purely formalist theories.

Morris' work remained true to his original purpose throughout his career. Although his painting and sculpture passed through various phases, there is more consistency than diversity in his oeuvre. Thus *Pivot*, a work from 1964, exhibits many of the same characteristics which Morris described in a 1941 article, in which he stated that his compositions ". . . are most frequently set in motion by a series of movements in opposition. . . ,"citing as an example a movement between two weighted areas which seem to have split apart (*Partisan Review*, p. 407). This describes the basic design of *Pivot*, where two large, dominant white shapes appear to have separated from one another. A sense of movement, of the pivot, is generated by semi-circular forms which swing about the white forms. Other

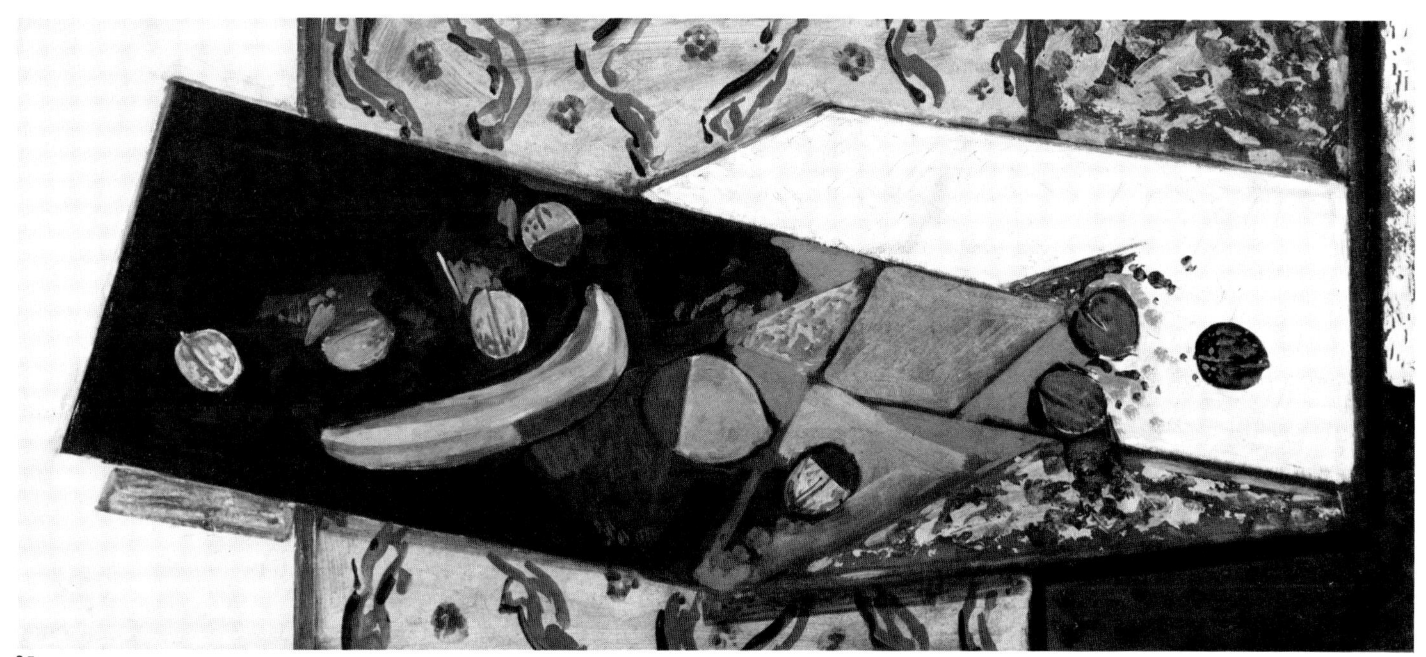
25

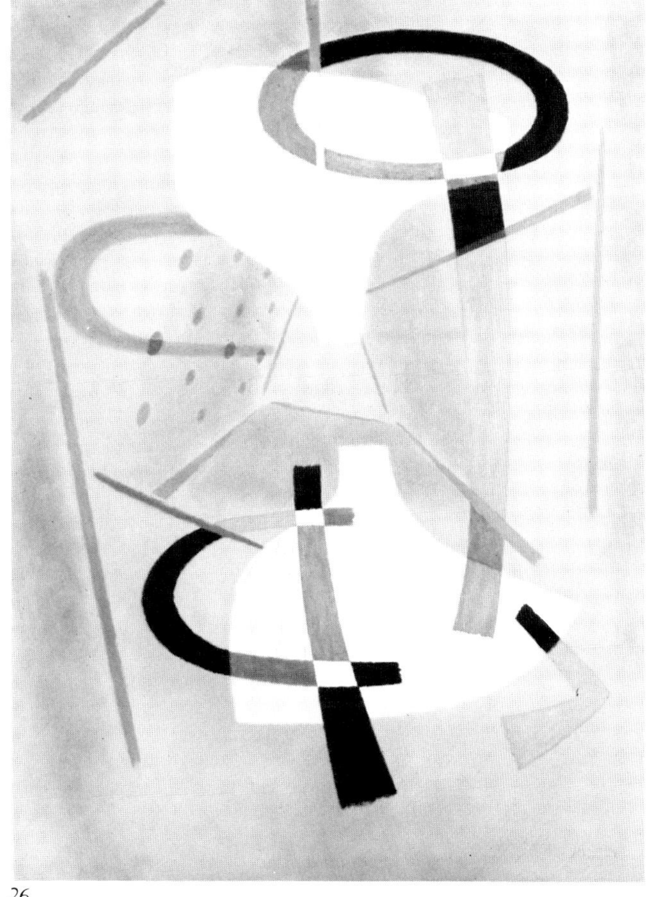
26

forms, such as the inward pointing lines, further the impression of movement about a central focus. All of this movement is, however, very controlled: even the outer edges of the composition are contained by lines which serve almost as a frame within the frame.

The three-dimensionality of space and form in this composition was a common feature of Morris' works of the fifties and sixties. The space seems to recede deeply in the center of the canvas, with all of the lines and forms moving in towards a central triangle, and with the blue background gradually changing from dark to light.

L.C.

Ashton, Dore. *George L. K. Morris: abstract art of the 1930's.* New York: Hirschl & Adler Galleries, Inc., 1974.

Hoopes, Donelson F. *George L. K. Morris.* Washington, D.C.: Corcoran Gallery of Art, 1965.

Morris, George L. K. "On the Mechanics of Abstract Painting." *Partisan Review,* vol. 8, no. 5, September October 1941, pp. 403–417.

WALTER MURCH (b. 1907)

27. MEDLEY, c. 1950–51

Oil on canvas
27 x 20 (68.6 x 50.8)
Signed upper right: *Walter Murch*
Whitney Museum of American Art

The discovery of Walter Tandy Murch by art critics came long after he was well established as a commerical artist. Born in 1907, Murch studied at the Ontario College of Art in Toronto under Arthur Lismer and J. E. D. McDonald, two of the best contemporary Canadian artists of the period. In 1927 Murch went to New York, where he found a job as a designer for a stained glass company. He continued to study art at the Art Students League but quit after a year, disappointed by the teaching at the famous school. Through the League, however, he heard about Arshile Gorky, who taught at the Grand Central School of Art. When Gorky quit Grand Central at the end of Murch's first semester, Murch continued to study with him privately until 1931, when he could no longer afford it. In the same year, Murch left the stained glass company and went to work in the art department at Lord and Taylor's, while at the same time working as a freelance illustrator. By 1936 he had enough freelance commissions to quit the store, and for the next fourteen years he painted murals for restaurants and apartment houses, magazine advertisements for companies, and cover illustrations.

When Murch's still lifes were exhibited—first at the Wakefield Gallery in 1941, and in later years at the Betty Parsons Gallery—they received cursory critical notice. Margaret Breuning, writing in 1949, commented on the "mortuary atmosphere" in which "the fish is mounted; the bird is dead; the eggs appear to have experienced a long life; the lemons, pear and potato suggest a tedious existence on the studio shelf" (Breuning, p. 21). Critics also remarked that fruit, such as the lemon in *Medley,* was treated in the same manner as machinery. Unlike other artists in the explosive era of Abstract Expressionism, Murch did not change his style to any great degree until 1962, when he began to include in his pictures objects like coats and hats, which had a more obvious connection with human beings.

Discussing painting, Murch stated that "to reduce the subject to the way it is reduced in an abstract painting permits the artist to emphasize the poetry. To force out poetry, this is my job" (Gray, p. 84). Using drawings which he altered by wrinkling or soaking them, Murch would plan his compositions. After coating the canvas with Duco or lead white, the artist scored the surface to break up the plane. Paint could then be applied with a hand, a rag, or a knife, as well as with a brush. "I want to put paint on—like Pollock did—and see what happens," Murch once explained (Browne, p. 38). The titles of the paintings were generally added later; he would often adopt a title based on someone else's reaction to the work.

Painted in 1954, *Medley* may have suggested a musical theme to a gallery visitor. Like so many Murch paintings, this work depicts a machine that does not work, surrounded by seemingly unrelated objects. It is a mouldering kind of still life, where strange combinations of things languish together gathering dust. The cool stillness of Murch's assemblages recalls Chardin's calm arrangements of fruit and flowers. In Walter Murch's paintings the objects have a personal rather than a universal significance; the viewer wonders why a lemon was placed just so, in such strange company.

G.O.

Breuning, Margaret. "Fifty-Seventh Street in Review: Textured Still Lifes." *The Art Digest,* vol. 23, 15 January 1949, p. 21.

Browne, Rosalind. "Short-Range Astronomy." *Art News,* vol. 64, January 1966, pp. 37–39.

Gray, Cleve. "Walter Murch Modern Alchemist." *Art in America,* vol. 51, no. 3, 1963, pp. 80–85.

Robbins, Daniel. *Walter Murch: A Retrospective Exhibition.* Providence: Rhode Island School of Design, 1966.

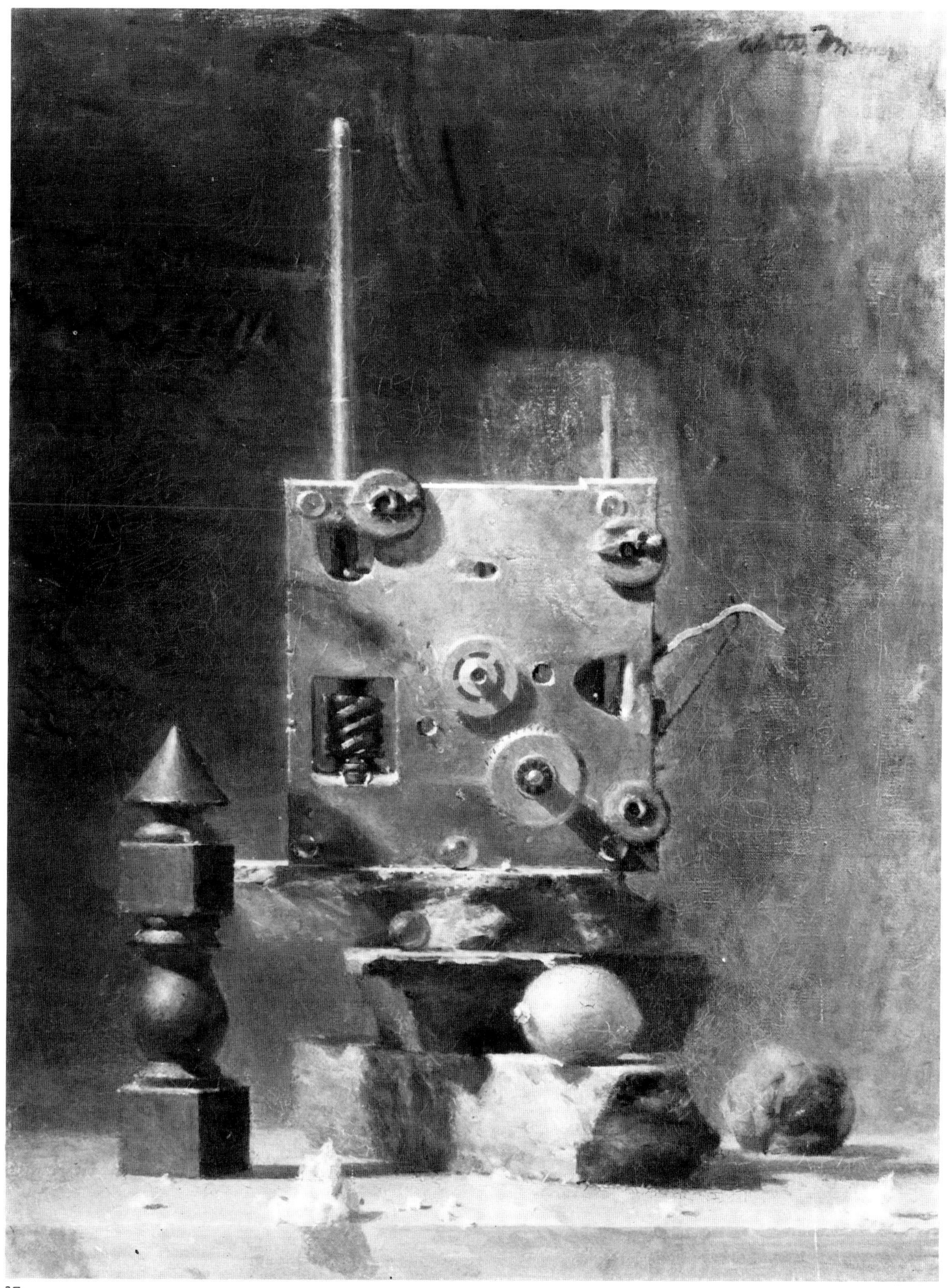

27

DAVID PARK (1911–1960)

28. RIVERBANK, 1956

Oil on canvas
57 11/16 x 68 (146.5 x 172.8)
Signed and dated lower right: *Park 56*
Williams College Museum of Art

David Park was one of the most important painters in a style of figurative abstraction that developed in California in the late 1940s as a direct answer to the incoming influence of the New York school. Born in Boston in 1911, Park was bright but fiercely independent in thought, and never did well in school. Painting came early to him as a way of satisfying his intellectual curiosity without the need for other people. By his teens Park was visiting members of his family out west, who were concerned for his future. In the 1930s he lived and worked in San Francisco, raised a family, and painted murals for the WPA until 1935, when he accepted a teaching position in Boston. But by the beginning of World War II he was back in California, and after the war he became involved once more as a teacher with the California School of Fine Art. His colleagues included the painters Hassel Smith, Elmer Bischoff, Mark Rothko and Clyfford Still. It was an important time for his art, and he painted under the influence of the New York school.

But it was not to last. In 1949 he destroyed almost all his Abstract Expressionist paintings and began to reintroduce the figure in his work. *Riverbank*, painted in 1956 at the height of his power, indicates the direction that his art was to take. In 1954 both Bischoff and Diebenkorn began to paint in a figurative manner, and it is instructive to compare their works in the exhibition with Park's. The style is a challenging one. Park paints with a full palette; dominating colors (in this case a strong green) are strengthened by broad, flat strokes of paint which achieve pictorial illusion in terms of form but at the expense of realism. Park's figures, like Cézanne's, are defined by strong light, broad color and open strokes. No traditional elements of perspective are used; through overlap of forms and juxtaposition of color, Park gives a sure sense of space. Park's aggressive paint style became controversial, then influential, and finally famous. His death from cancer in 1960 prevented him from a fuller realization of his vision.

R.S.

Howe, Thomas. *David Park: Recent Paintings*. New York: Staempfli Art Gallery, 1959.

Mills, Paul. *David Park*. San Francisco: Maxwell Galleries, 1970.

Turnbull, Betty. *David Park 1911–1960*. Newport Beach, California: Newport Harbor Art Museum, 1977.

PHILIP PEARLSTEIN (b. 1924)

29. TWO FEMALE NUDES WITH RED DRAPE, 1970

Oil on canvas
60 x 72 (152.4 x 182.9)
Signed and dated lower right: *Pearlstein 70*
Williams College Museum of Art

Born in Pittsburgh in 1924, Philip Pearlstein received a B.F.A. from Carnegie-Mellon University in 1949 and then moved to New York City where he lived with his old schoolmate, Andy Warhol. For the next seven years Pearlstein created layouts and diagrams for industrial trade catalogues. He completed his education in 1955 at the Institute of Fine Arts, New York University, and that same year had his first one-man show at the Tanager Gallery, New York.

The year 1958 was the most decisive of Pearlstein's career. Prior to that year he had painted Abstract Expressionist landscapes and natural forms—very much under the influence of Chaim Soutine's violent mountain landscapes, but with a painting process that revealed his innate fascination with structure. In 1958, however, he revolted against the totalitarian rule of Abstract Expressionism and began figure painting. At the same time he quit his graphic design work, transferring to his canvases the precision and strong compositional designs that had dominated his graphic work.

The composition of *Two Female Nudes with Red Drape* is a tight, centrifugal design. With an eye like a camera, Pearlstein wilfully crops the figures at head and mid-calf to neutralize the humanity of his subject. The cropped image, which appears incomplete, interrupts the models' physical presence and stresses the formal elements of their poses. The picture plane is thereby flattened, with an equal tension applied to all edges. The three shadows on the left edge, cast by the hard electric lights, radiate from the body. The shadows facilitate modeling but also create a flattening pattern; as forms, they are repeated variations of themselves, echoing shapes. Thus, light creates an artistic tension of figure versus pattern, volume versus abstraction.

In this painting, structure—mass and perspective—dominates. Pearlstein's empirical approach to detail, the veins of the model's hand, and his objective attention to anatomy and modeling create a monumental plasticity. The strong diagonals of the models' legs recede to a single vantage point. The

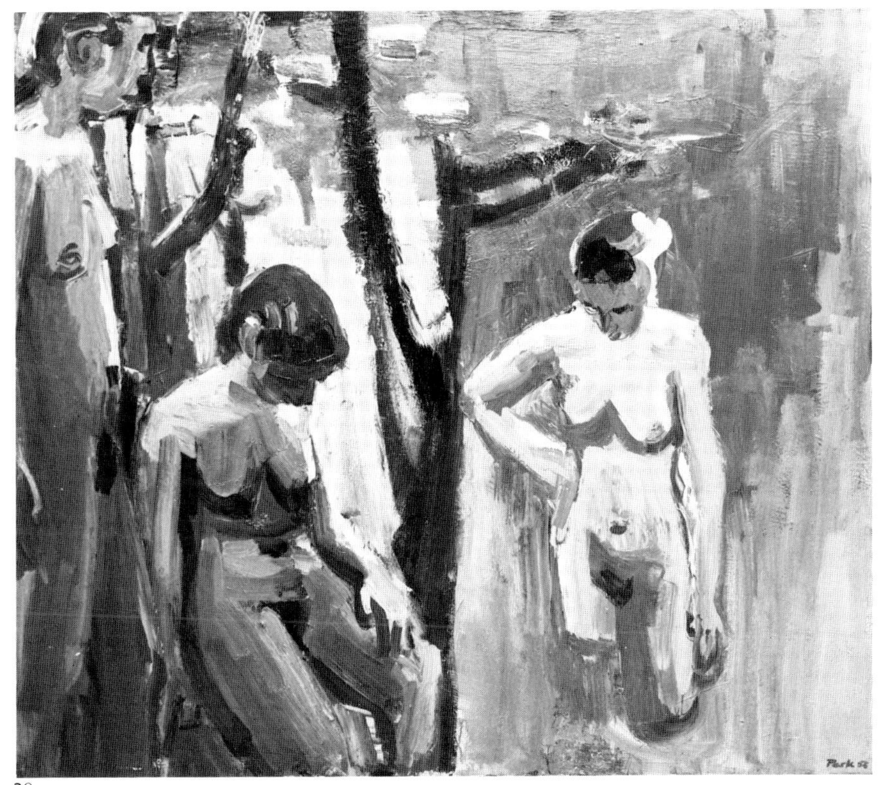

28

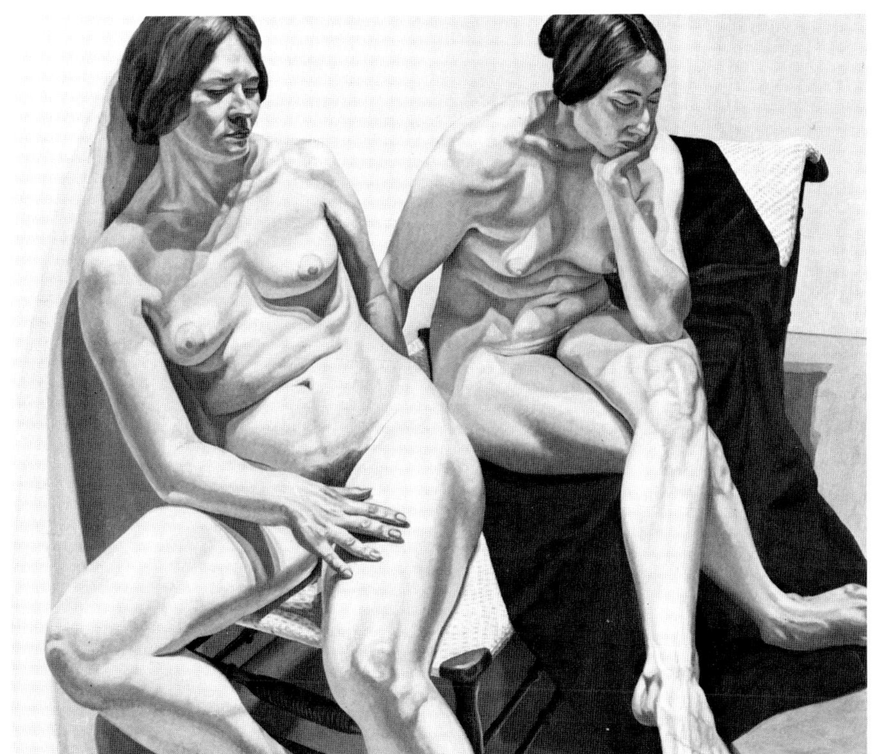
29

foreshortened forms illustrate a deep three-dimensional space, but the surface patterns of their shapes oppose the recession and suggest a two-dimensional activity. The work exemplifies Pearlstein's commitment to formalism. His subject is *not* two nudes; rather, a heroic concept of mass and plasticity and the tension of an active surface.

J.H.

Midgette, Willard. "Philip Pearlstein: The Naked Truth." *Art News*, vol. 66 October 1967, 54–55.
Nochlin, Linda. "The Ugly American." *Art News*, vol. 69, September 1970, 55–57.
Schwartz, Ellen. "A Conversation with Philip Pearlstein." *Art in America*, vol. 59, October 1971, 50–57.

FAIRFIELD PORTER (1907–1975)

30. SCREEN PORCH, 1964

Oil on canvas
79½ x 79½ (202.0 x 202.0)
Signed and dated upper right: *Fairfield Porter 1964*
Whitney Museum of American Art

Fairfield Porter, born in Winnetka, Illinois in 1907, was educated at Harvard and then studied at the Art Students League in New York with Thomas Hart Benton and Boardman Robinson. In 1949 Porter and his wife, the poet Anne Channing, moved to Southhampton, Long Island, where the artist could paint the landscape around him and still be close to New York. Most of Porter's paintings are landscapes and interiors in Southampton and in Maine, where the Porters spent their summers.

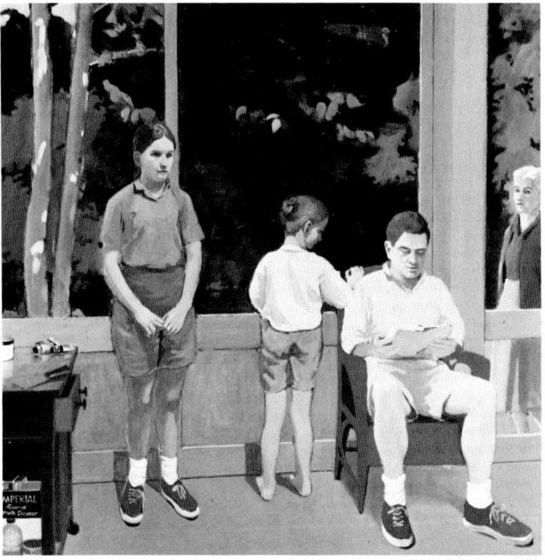

30

Two concepts, abstraction and intimism, are evident in *Screen Porch*, a large painting more than six feet high and six feet wide. Dated 1964, it is a group portrait: the seated man is James Schuyler, the woman Porter's wife, and the girls his children. They are posed across the width of the canvas; there is little contact mentally or physically among them. Typical of Porter's work is the equivalence of the figures and the space they occupy. The screen porch and the trees are just as important as the figures. The strong verticals of the trees, the standing figures and the porch are balanced by the horizontals of the wide floor, wall and mass of foliage. The three foreground figures, with their visible black outlines, look as though they are pasted onto the canvas. The viewer is confused and unsettled trying to understand who these people are and and how they are related. Porter fits into the history of modern art in several ways. His work can be related to Impressionism and Intimism; his interiors especially link him with Vuillard's works. Yet Porter can also be connected to the Abstract Expressionists in his way of seeing and conceiving a picture. One of the most intriguing aspects of his painting is the design of the picture surface. In *Screen Porch*, the colors are arranged in mosaic-like patterns, lying flat against each other; the vibrant purples and pinks of the girls' clothes seem to float on the surface. The white pools of paint on the birch trees and the abstract treatment of the leaves and foliage further heighten the viewer's awareness of the surface. Yet this flat surface, filled with Porter's unique bland light, can still project a feeling of deep space; the eye notices the heavy green and black brushstrokes of the foliage in the center, but also sees depth in that space. The painting does what an Impressionist work was meant to do and what an abstract painting often does: the viewer is conscious of the surface and the paint itself, but also notices real depth and limitless space drawing the eye back into the canvas.

M.S.

Benedikt, Michael. "Fairfield Porter; Minimum of Melodrama." *Art News*, March 1964, pp. 36–7.
Cummings, Paul. "Fairfield Porter: Interview." *Journal of Archives of American Art*, vol. 12, no. 2, November 1972, pp. 10–21.
Downes, Rackstraw. "Fairfield Porter: The Painter as Critic." *Art Journal*, vol. 37, no. 4, Summer 1978, pp. 306–12.
Schuyler, James. "Immediacy is the Message; Fairfield Porter." *Art News*, March 1967, pp. 32–3.

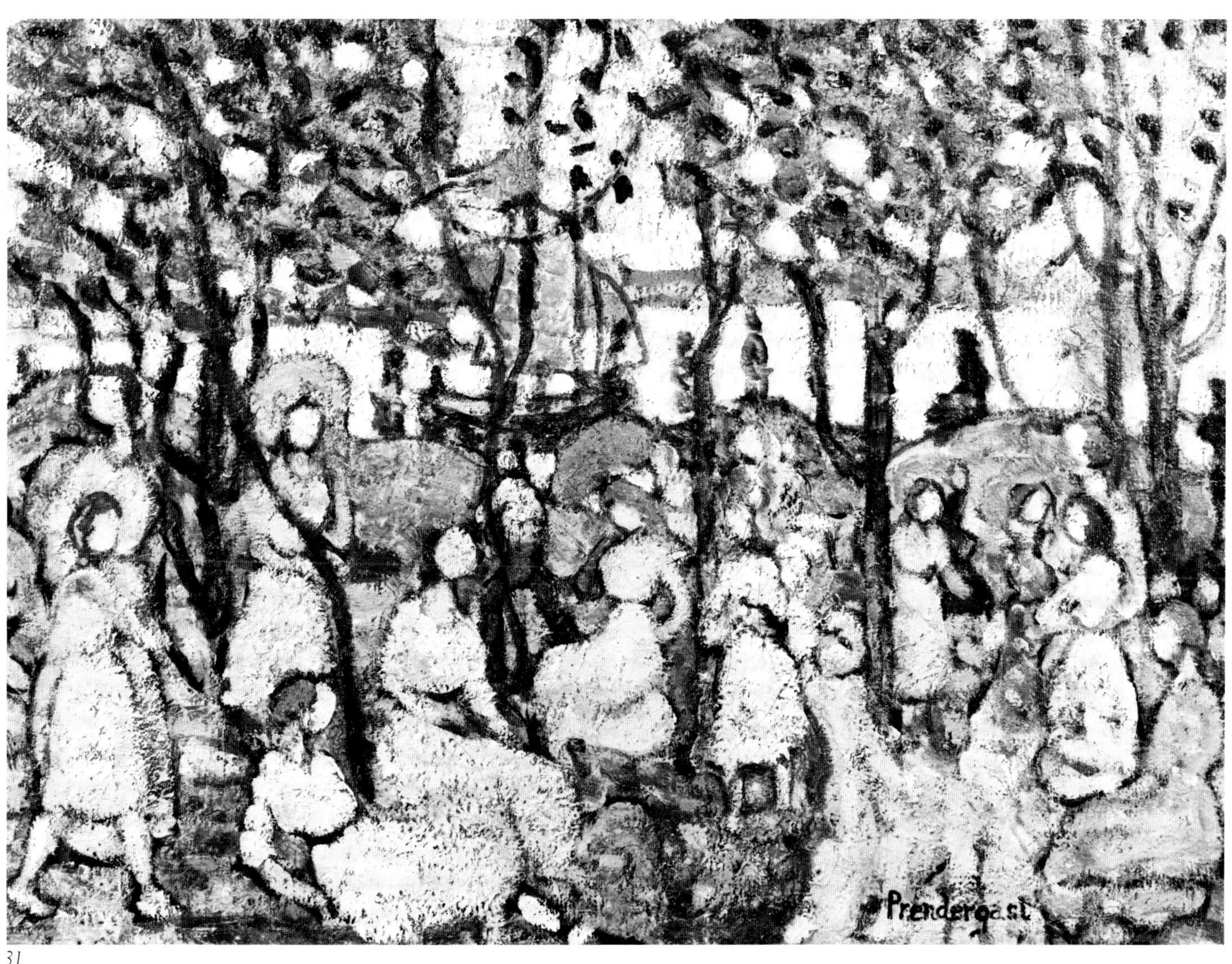

31

MAURICE PRENDERGAST (1859–1954)

31. SUMMER'S DAY, 1916–18

Oil on canvas
20¼ x 28½ (51.4 x 72.4)
Signed lower right: *Prendergast*
Whitney Museum of American Art

Even during his lifetime Maurice Prendergast was heralded as the "first American modernist." A New England artist born in Newfoundland, Prendergast created a vast oeuvre in oil, watercolor and monotype. He began his artistic career modestly as a watercolorist and created a number of sparkling, luminous works; he then went on to develop a less realistic style which emphasized the pattern on the surface. His development does not, however, follow a straight path, and even now surprising variations in his style are being discovered.

Already beyond his thirtieth birthday when he began to study at the Académie Julian in 1892, Prendergast became friends with a fellow art student, James Wilson Morrice, who knew Paris intimately and was no doubt responsible for Prendergast's exposure to Cézanne, as well as his later interest in Matisse and the Fauves. Numerous artistic sources for Prendergast's style can be named, but it is a combination of the influences of Puvis de Chavannes, Paul Signac, Pierre Bonnard, Henri Matisse and Paul Cézanne (Prendergast is credited as the first American artist to understand and assimilate Cézanne's contribution to art), as well as numerous lesser-known American painters, that makes his style unique.

After his return from Paris in 1895, Prendergast began exhibiting watercolors in annual exhibitions. His work did not go unnoticed in these vast yearly shows; both the Art Institute of Chicago and the Cincinnati Art Museum held special exhibitions of his work in 1900 and 1901 respectively. William Macbeth, a gallery owner in New York who was to become prominent as the agent for many modernist painters, was aware of Prendergast's work by 1899. Through him Prendergast met many other New York painters, including Robert Henri and Arthur B. Davies. Along with these, Prendergast became part of the famous "Eight" whose joint exhibition at Macbeth's gallery in 1908 was a direct challenge to the National Academy's juried shows.

In his later oil paintings, such as *Summer's Day*, Prendergast used a dry brush and thick paint, building up the surface of the canvas by adding layers of color one upon the other. The short staccato brushstrokes give the surface of these works a texture that has often been compared to woven tapestries. An air of stillness pervades *Summer's Day*; the figures all seem to be caught mid-way through a gesture that they will never complete. None of the figures has a face; the consistent treatment of the subjects, be they trees or people, gives the impression that the artist was more interested in the relationship of the shapes than in human personalities. This way of seeing recalls Cézanne's famous dictum to look at nature in terms of geometric shapes. In many of his later works Prendergast achieves a near-perfect balance in the relationship of shapes and colors which echo across the surface. Coupled with the texture of the painting, this gives these late oils a vibrance and life in themselves. *Summer's Day* is an outstanding example of a work which shows the culmination of Maurice Prendergast's explorations in paint.

G.O.

Green, Eleanor. *Maurice Prendergast*. College Park, Maryland: University of Maryland Art Gallery, 1976.

Ownes, Gwendolyn. *Watercolors by Maurice Prendergast from New England Collections*. Williamstown, Massachusetts: Sterling and Francine Clark Art Institute, 1978.

Rhys, Hedley. *Maurice Prendergast 1859–1954*. Boston: Museum of Fine Arts, 1960.

LARRY RIVERS (b. 1923)

32. BERDIE IN A RED SHAWL, 1953

Oil on canvas
53 x 65 (134.6 x 165.1)
Unsigned; dated label on verso.
Whitney Museum of American Art

Born in the Bronx in 1923, Larry Rivers became a jazz musician, playing the saxophone professionally beginning in 1940. In the middle of that decade he began experimenting with painting and in 1947 began formal study under Hans Hofmann. Rivers continued to study with Hofmann through the summer of 1948 and then took classes at New York University with the aim of becoming a teacher of painting himself. In 1949 he had his first one-man exhibition at the Jane Street Gallery. In his review of Rivers' exhibition Clement Greenberg commented on the obvious influence of Bonnard (whose retrospective Rivers had seen the previous year at the Museum of Modern Art) but concluded that this young artist had great potential (Greenberg, pp. 453–4). The next year, following a trip to Europe,

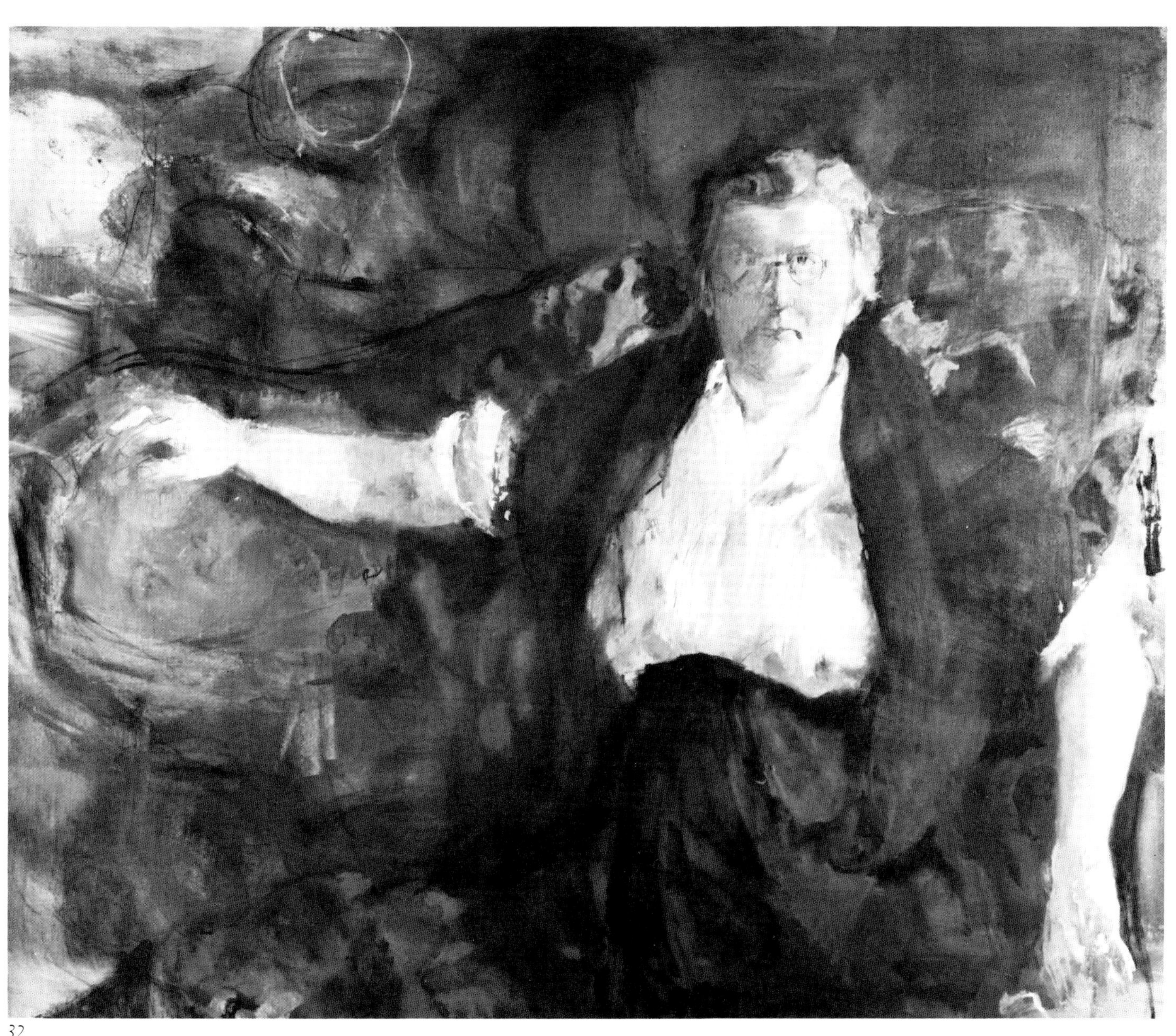
32

Rivers decided to devote all of his time to painting. Of crucial importance were the friendships he made in this period; poets Kenneth Koch and Frank O'Hara, painters Franz Kline and Helen Frankenthaler were all to influence his work. Grand dame for the circle of young poets and painters was Berdie Burger, the mother of Rivers' ex-wife, with whom the artist and his two sons shared a house.

In the early fifties, public controversy began over Rivers' works. In an era when new paintings were abstract, Rivers was painting distorted versions of famous paintings and realistic portraits of his family and friends, often nude and looking unappealing and absurd. It became apparent that Rivers, like Matisse, knew how to reduce the object to quintessential elements of paint and line.

At first glance, *Berdie in a Red Shawl* (1953) appears to be a straightforward clothed portrait of the artist's ex-mother-in-law. However, a closer examination reveals faces outlined sideways at Berdie's right, one below her outstretched arm and the other in the upper left corner of the canvas. The soft blurred forms draw one back to seek more traces in the other corners, but to no avail. Rivers' painting becomes a complex tapestry of suggestion. He tells us, with expressive brushstrokes and patches of paint, only as much as he feels it is necessary for us to know.

G.O.

Greenberg, Clement. "Art." *The Nation*, vol. 168, 16 April 1949.

Larry Rivers. Waltham, Mass.: Brandeis University, Poses Institute of Fine Arts, 1965.

Myers, John Bernard. "The Terrible Larry Rivers." *Artforum*, vol. 16, October 1977, pp. 50–55.

Soby, James Thrall. "The Fine Arts: Interview with Larry Rivers." *Saturday Review*, vol. 38, 3 September 1955, pp. 23–24.

MORGAN RUSSELL (1886–1953)

33. SYNCHROMY NO. 6 (One part of three-part Synchromy), c. 1922–23

Oil on canvas
10 ¼ x 13 (26.0 x 33.0)
Signed lower right: *Morgan Russell*
Whitney Museum of American Art

Born in New York in 1886, Morgan Russell studied at the Art Students League in 1906 and also studied painting with Robert Henri. Aided by a small allowance from Gertrude Vanderbilt Whitney, Russell left for Paris in 1908. There he was drawn to styles which favored color: he admired Cézanne in particular, recognizing the brilliance of the artist's method for building up form through planes of color; he was likewise drawn to the vivid colors of Fauvism and by 1911 was producing works closely related to that style.

In 1912 Russell saw the Futurist exhibition at the Bernheim-Jeune Gallery, which no doubt encouraged him to begin viewing his own thoughts and theories as the foundation for a new movement. However, it was not until the following year that Synchromism was officially founded with the opening of an exhibition of works by Russell and Stanton MacDonald-Wright at Der Neue Kunstsalon in Munich. The majority of the paintings were based on figurative compositions, and all were highly charged with brilliant color, a trait which was to become basic to Synchromism. As the style was perfected in the following months, color ultimately came to assume form and the works became ever more abstract.

By 1914 Russell's ideas had solidified and he was painting in a powerful style. In 1917 he settled in the south of France and then, in 1921, moved to Burgundy. For a brief period after 1922 he returned to painting Synchromies, producing a series of works known as "Eidos," from the Greek for "form" or "shape."

Synchromy No. 6 (One Part of a Three-Part Synchromy) dates from Russell's last experiments with Synchromism. The bright colors recall the earlier works, but the forms are less surely defined and seem to float in a vague space. The rich impasto gives the surface of the painting a strongly tactile quality. The question of multi-part Synchromies is a vexing one, for it is difficult to determine what significance these had for Russell. He had painted a *Four-Part Synchromy, No. 7* in 1914–15 (Whitney Museum of American Art), and a number of small studies on transparent paper which were meant to be shown with light projecting through them. The latter are in clearly divided sections, not unlike the frames of movie film. It seems possible that Russell may have painted his small late oils for a similar purpose, perhaps to be arranged and rearranged in exploring different color sequences.

F.K.

Levin, Gail. "Morgan Russell's Notebooks: An American Avant-Garde Painter in Paris." *Canadian Art Review*, vol. 3, 1976, pp. 73–87.

____. *Synchromism and American Color Abstraction 1910–1925*. New York: Whitney Museum of American Art, 1978.

____. "Synchromism: The State of the Scholarship—Past, Present and Future." *Arts Magazine*, vol. 53, no. 1, September 1978, pp. 131–35.

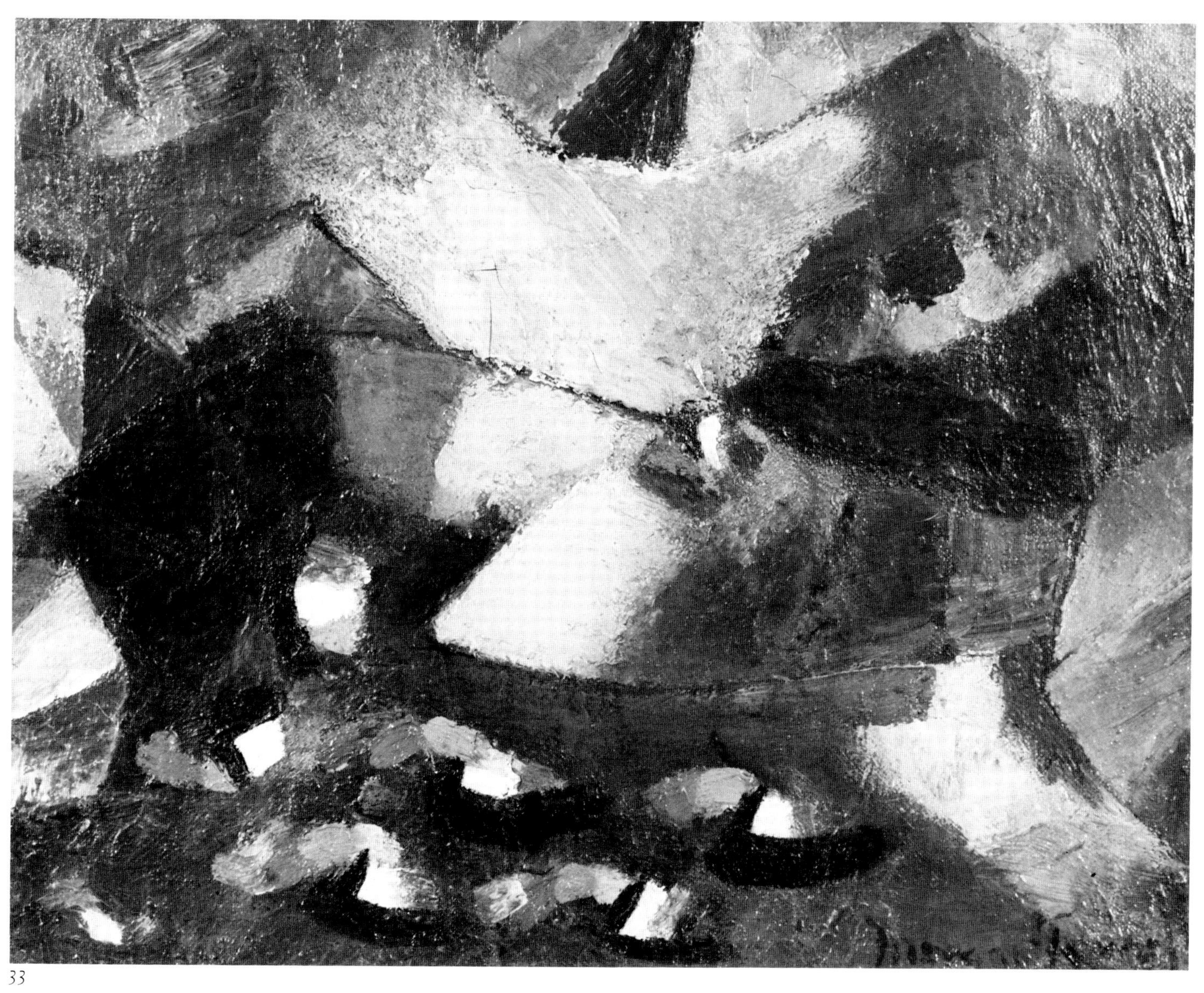

33

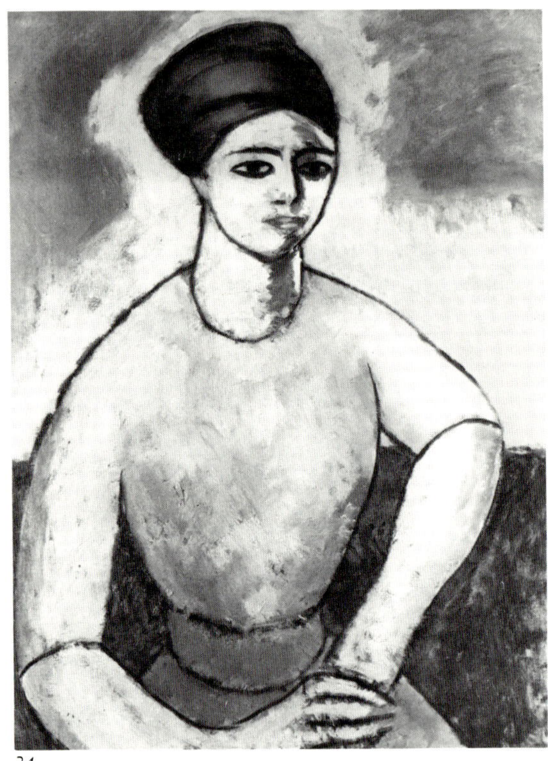
34

MORTON LIVINGSTON SCHAMBERG (1881–1918)

34. STUDY OF A GIRL (Fanette Reider), c. 1911

Oil on canvas
30 7/8 x 22 7/8 (78.4 x 58.1)
Signed and dated on verso
Williams College Museum of Art

Morton Livingston Schamberg was one of the most important innovators in early 20th-century American painting, but his creativity was cut short by his untimely death at age 37. Born in 1881 into an affluent and conservative Philadelphia family, Schamberg enrolled in the Pennsylvania Academy of Fine Arts in 1903. There he studied painting under William Merritt Chase, whose summer study tours of Europe instilled in Schamberg an appreciation of the beauty of the Old Masters. Upon graduation from the academy in 1906 Schamberg went to Europe, where he observed contemporary artistic trends and developed enthusiasm for the Fauves and the Cubists; soon after his return to Philadelphia in 1909 he painted *Study of a Girl (Fanette Reider)*. He had his first one-man exhibition in 1910, and in 1913 five of his paintings (including *Study of a Girl*) were exhibited in the Armory Show. His work from this period shows the influence of Cézanne, Matisse and the Fauves, as well as his old teacher, Chase.

Schamberg painted many portraits of Fanette Reider, a young woman he might have married had he been able to offer her financial security. She remembers Schamberg fondly: "He made many, many pictures of me, always changing the youthful peaches and cream complexion to citron and verdigris!" (MacAgy, p. 40) The *Study of a Girl* of 1911 is certainly one of the most startling of Schamberg's portrayals of his friend. The picture is dominated by brilliant Fauvist colors: deep green, blue, yellow, and bits of red sometimes blend and sometimes contrast with each other. The body is abstracted so that every angle becomes a curve and ovals repeat themselves throughout the canvas, yet this roundness is two-dimensional. The flatness of the painting is emphasized by the wide, sharply contrasting blue outline of the girl, which denies the attempts at strong green shading. Bold mask-like eyes set below a dark blue turban are reminiscent of some of the African-inspired faces of Picasso.

As one of the early attempts by Americans at painting in the style of the Paris vanguard, *Study of a Girl* must have startled visitors to the Armory Show, but the painter's effort becomes even more dramatic when it is remembered that Schamberg lived, worked and exhibited in artistically conservative Philadelphia. Seen in the context of Schamberg's oeuvre, this painting is really an experiment with the lessons learned in Europe.

T.W.

MacAgy, Douglas. "Five Rediscovered from the Lost Generation," *Art News*, Summer 1960, pp. 39ff.
Powell, Earl A. "Morton Livingston Schamberg: The Machine as Icon." *Arts Magazine*, vol. 51, May 1977, pp. 122–23.
Wolf, Ben. *Morton Livingston Schamberg*. Philadelphia: University of Pennsylvania Press, 1963.

CHARLES SHEELER (1883–1965)

35. ON A CONNECTICUT THEME, 1958

Oil on canvas
19 1/2 x 29 1/2 (49.5 x 74.9)
Signed and dated lower right: *Sheeler 1958*
Whitney Museum of American Art

Charles Sheeler began his artistic career in 1900 with three years of study at the School of Industrial Art in Philadelphia, followed by three years as one of William Merritt Chase's favorite students at the Pennsylvania Academy of the Fine Arts. A trip to

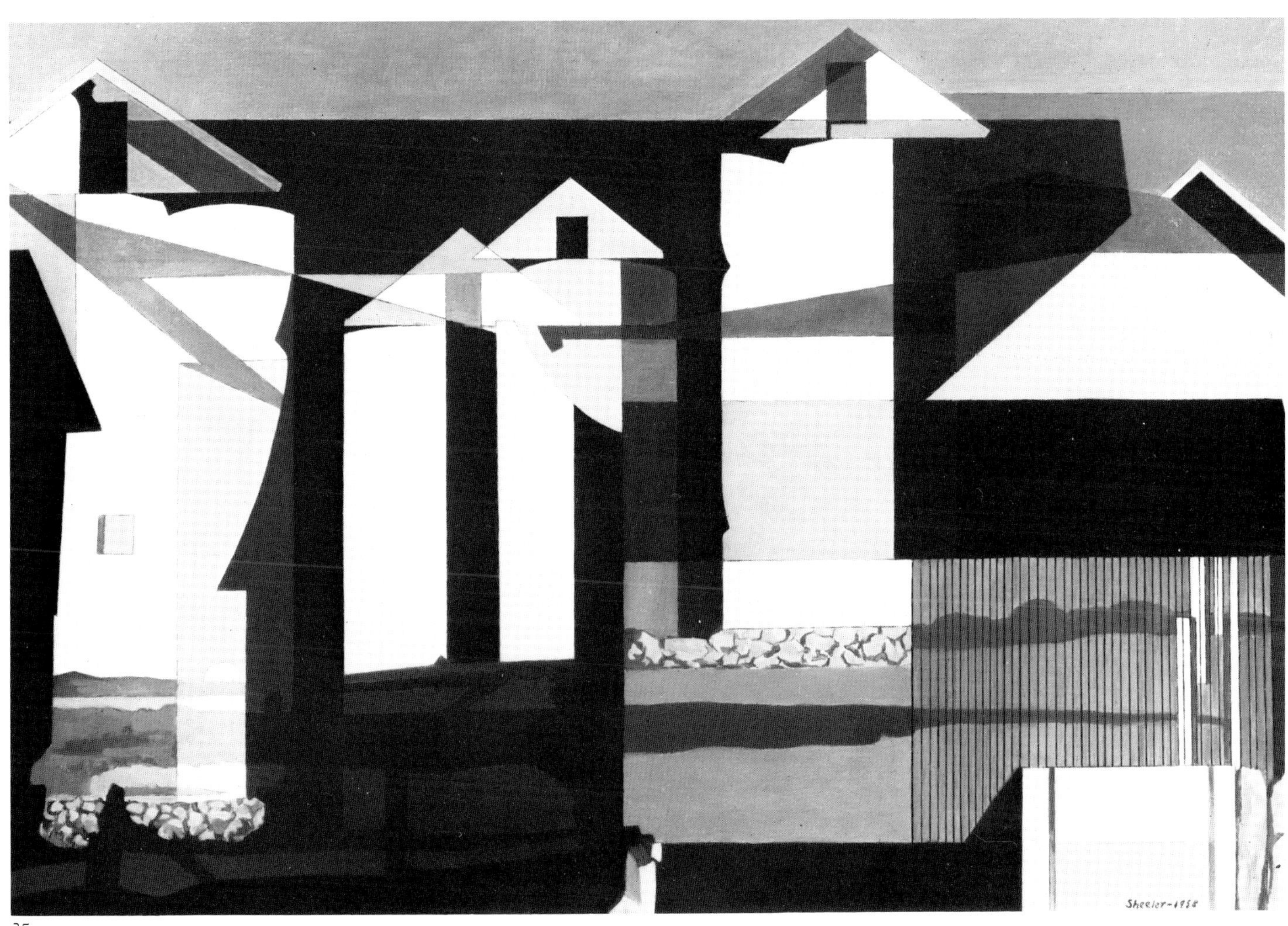

35

Europe in 1900 with Morton Schamberg exposed Sheeler to the more recent abstractions of Cézanne, Picasso and Matisse, and produced a drastic stylistic transition in his work; his still lifes and interiors of the next decade reflect an interest in formal relationships between shapes, rather than in the extra-pictorial connotations of the subject. In the 1920s Sheeler realized the potential of his art as a didactic tool to illustrate the inherent abstract order and beauty of objects and motifs in a meticulously realistic style. These works required months of careful planning as well as extremely smooth, even paint application so that no texture would distract the viewer from the order and clarity of his design.

In 1946 Sheeler's paintings began to show bright colors and superimposed images, as opposed to his more tonal, hyper-realistic work of the thirties. While value remained paramount in his choice of color, hue gained greatly in importance. These changes may have resulted in part from new developments in color photography, which Sheeler used to produce preliminary "sketches" of his motifs.

On a Connecticut Theme is typical of Sheeler's late work in its repetition of a familiar motif in his oeuvre, the rural barn. These works tend to be compilations and distillations of characteristic views of the motif, in this case, the blank barn walls, the peaked roofs, the suggestion of silo shapes, and fragments of stone walls. Except in the surprisingly realistic sections of stone wall, almost all texture and detail have been abstracted, leaving recognizable shapes seemingly superimposed upon one another.

The colors of the painting seem somewhat arbitrary: the green of the grass and the purple of the shadows are but distantly related to the colors of the original forms. Indeed, Sheeler's green has as much to do with the other colors and shapes in the painting as with the color of real grass. His working method in this period was to experiment with tempera on plexiglas, which allowed him to make changes simply by wiping the glass with a wet sponge; once satisfied, he would transfer the design to a larger canvas.

The musical reference of the title is common in Sheeler's later works. It not only suggests the repetition of familiar images within the painting, much as a musical theme is treated in a sonata or rondo, but also the recurrence of this subject within Sheeler's oeuvre.

L.V.

Charles Sheeler. Washington: National Collection of Fine Arts, Smithsonian Institution, 1968.

Dochterman, Lillian N. "The Stylistic Development of the Work of Charles Sheeler." PhD Dissertation, State University of Iowa, 1963.

Friedman, Martin. *Charles Sheeler.* New York: Watson-Guptill, 1975.

"Interview: Charles Sheeler Talks with Martin Friedman." *Archives of American Art Journal*, vol. 16, no. 4, 1976, pp. 15–19.

JOSEPH STELLA (1877–1946)

36. BROOKLYN BRIDGE, 1919

Charcoal on paper
22¼ x 17⅞ (56.5 x 45.4)
Signed and dated upper right: *Joseph/Stella/1919*; lower right: *Joseph Stella/1919*
Williams College Museum of Art

Born and raised in a small hill town in southern Italy, Joseph Stella immigrated to New York in 1896. In 1897 he enrolled at the Art Students League, and from 1898 to 1900 he studied with William Merritt Chase at the New York School of Art. Although these three years were his only formal artistic training, an extended trip to Italy and France (1909–13) introduced Stella to Italian Futurism and French Orphism, and in particular the work of Robert Delaunay, with its bright and pulsating colors.

After returning to New York, Stella spent several years in Manhattan and then in 1917 moved to Williamsburg, Brooklyn, where he lived practically in the shadow of the Brooklyn Bridge. The bridge—with its striking interplay between the cobweb of diagonal steel cables and the strong verticality of the pylons, along with the glimpse of the Manhattan skyline through the two Gothic arches—provided a spectacular source of subject matter for early 20th-century painters and poets. For Stella it "had become an ever growing obsession ever since I had come to America" (*Transition*, p. 87), and the Bloedel sketch of 1919 is one of several preliminary ideas for his first painting of the structure.

When the painting, *Brooklyn Bridge* (New Haven, Yale University Art Gallery), was shown at the Bourgeois Galleries in April 1920, it was described as a "strangely modern and subjective presentation of the bridge, seen from within, literally and figuratively" (*Current Opinion*, pp. 832–33). With one exception, this symmetry becomes increasingly pronounced in Stella's five subsequent paintings of the bridge, where there is more emphasis on the vista of Manhattan and also a far more streamlined and less atmospheric quality. The asymmetrical exception is the *American Landscape* of c. 1929 (Minneapolis, Walker Art Center, illus. Jaffe, 1970, fig. 91), in which the cables veer off to the right, and the left arch is cut off. Even more chaotic in its composition, the Bloedel sketch seems to be the source for the Minneapolis work. There is even less sense of a

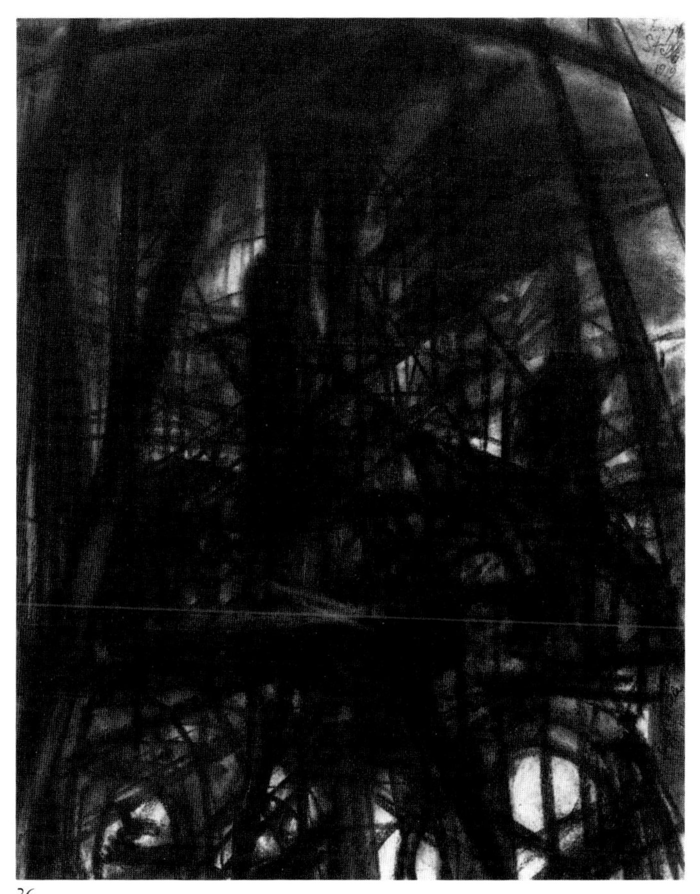
36

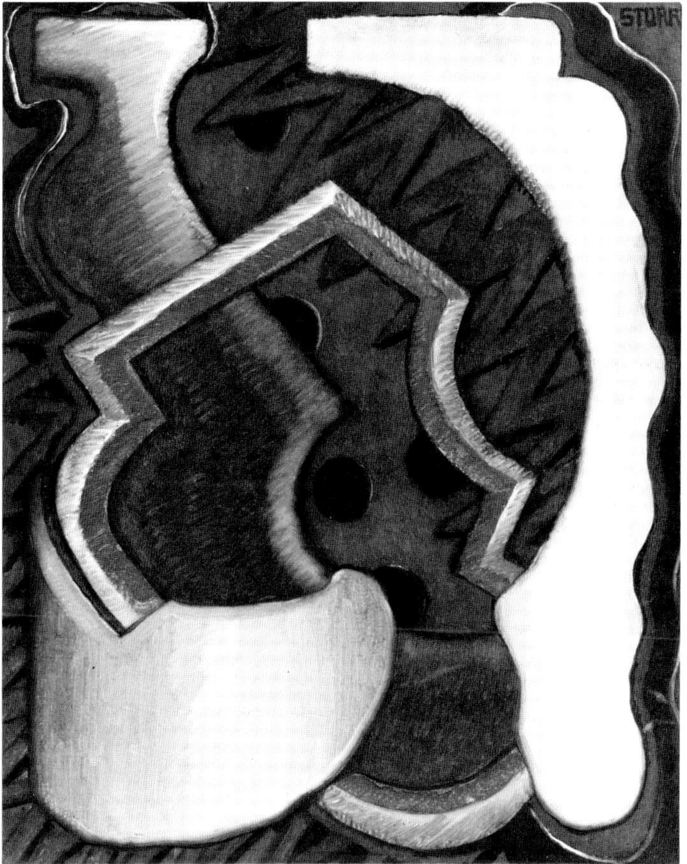

37

skyline in the distance, and the slashing cables entwine the arches. The dark quality of the sketch reflects the brooding side of Stella, who, despite his exclamations over the exciting artistic possibilities provided by the "monstrous steely bar" of New York, made frequent references to the city's gloomy metallic skies and general claustrophobic and prison-like atmosphere.

The Bloedel sketch must be seen in context with the different preliminary ideas for the *Brooklyn Bridge*. Its appearance reveals that Stella did more than simply foreshadow the Precisionist style, as is frequently thought when looking at the finished painting. Simultaneously attracted to clean-cut abstraction and an atmospheric realism, in this drawing Stella delineated his romantic vision of the Brooklyn Bridge as opposed to his later, more ordered and monumental interpretations.

L.G.

Baur, John I. H. *Joseph Stella*, New York: Whitney Museum of American Art, 1963.

Jaffe, Irma B. *Joseph Stella*. Cambridge: Harvard University Press, 1970.

Stella, Joseph. "The Brooklyn Bridge (A Page of My Life)." *Transition* 16–17, June 1929, pp. 86–88. Previously printed and distributed privately by Stella.

"A Subjective Version of the Brooklyn Bridge." *Current Opinion*, vol. 68, 1920, pp. 832 ff.

JOHN STORRS (1885–1956)

37. ABSTRACT IN BLUE AND GREEN, 1934

Oil on canvas
16¼ x 13 (41.3 x 33.0)
Signed upper right: *Storrs*
Whitney Museum of American Art

John Storrs was born in Chicago in 1885, the son of a successful architect. In 1910 he enrolled in the Pennsylvania Academy of the Fine Arts; the following year he went to Paris to study at the Académie Julian and the Ecole des Beaux Arts. A turning point in his career came in 1912 when he entered Rodin's studio, where he was encouraged to develop his own style. Following Rodin's death in 1917 Storrs, reportedly one of the master's favorite pupils, was asked to draw a final portrait of the great French sculptor.

By the late teens Storrs was beginning to experiment with a more streamlined style that anticipated Art Deco; in his sculptures he began to approach machine-like forms, perhaps in reaction to the burgeoning technology of the period. Storrs had by the mid-twenties developed a unique style of non-objective sculpture which recalled the stepped skyscraper forms of his native Chicago and New York. He was the first American sculptor to work with metals directly, and his inspired combinations of various materials in one work made him one of the most innovative sculptors of the period.

Storrs first began to paint seriously in 1930; his first painting show was held in 1931 in Chicago. Critical reaction was mixed, but reviewers did single out Storrs' use of color for praise. The more perceptive writers recognized that his concern for sculptural form clearly carried over into his paintings.

Storrs proved to be a remarkably varied painter, sometimes creating strictly defined geometrical fantasies, other times producing biomorphic abstractions which closely resemble Surrealist works. *Abstract in Blue and Green* from 1934 displays the curious hybrid forms that Storrs often favored in his paintings. The shapes loom large in the canvas with a convincing three-dimensionality. Like many other sculptors who painted, Storrs tended to define shapes crisply and clearly. But the space is vague, suggested only by the overlapping and intertwining of the various forms. Works such as this have a strangely moody and ominous quality, suggesting that Storrs was drawing on some deep inner source of inspiration. Unfortunately, he remained reluctant throughout his life to discuss his art. His wife once compared him to a chameleon, and his paintings reflect this enigmatic quality.

F.K.

Bryant, Edward. "Rediscovery: John Storrs." *Art in America*, vol. 57, no. 3, May-June 1969, pp. 66–71.

Davidson, Abraham A. "John Storrs, Early Sculptor of the Machine Age." *Artforum*, vol. 13, no. 3, November 1974, pp. 41–45.

Jewett, Eleanor. "Storrs, Cubist Sculptor, Takes up Brush," *The Arts Digest*, vol. 5, no. 13, 1 April 1931, p. 9 (reprinted from the *Chicago Daily Tribune*).

Kramer, Hilton. "The Return of John Storrs." In *The Age of the Avant-Garde: An Art Chronicle of 1956–1972*. New York: Farrar, Strauss and Giroux, 1973.

MARK TOBEY (1890–1976)

38. LANDSCAPE, 1957

Gouache on paper
5³⁄₁₆ x 14⅛ (13.2 x 35.9)
Signed and dated lower right: *Tobey 57*
Williams College Museum of Art

If the strength of art lies in its appeal to universal perception, then Mark Tobey was one of its most significant practitioners. Tobey's art involved a lifetime of universal commitment, an attitude toward creative expression that seemed timeless and without boundaries.

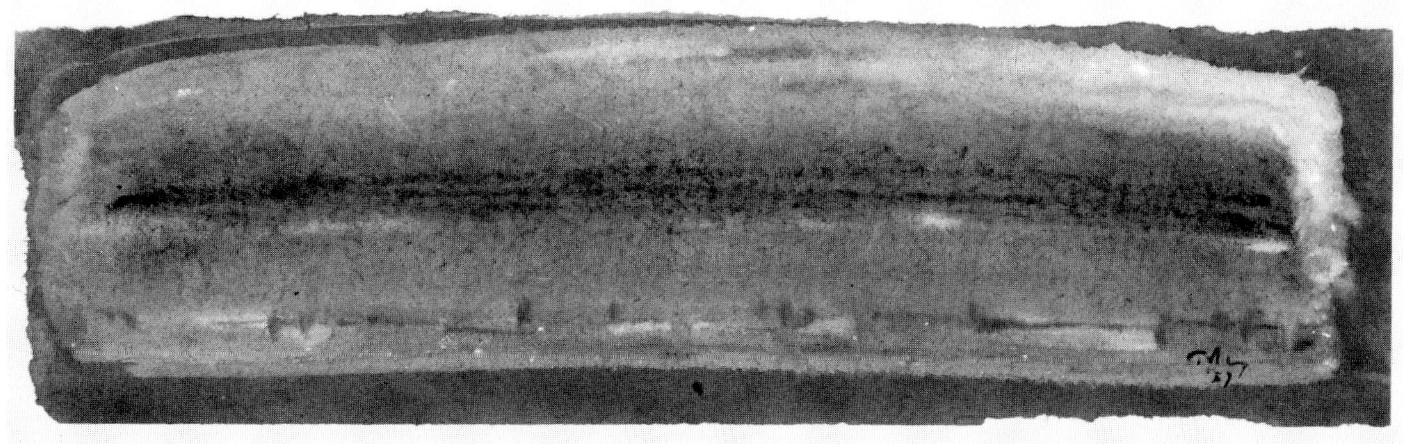

38

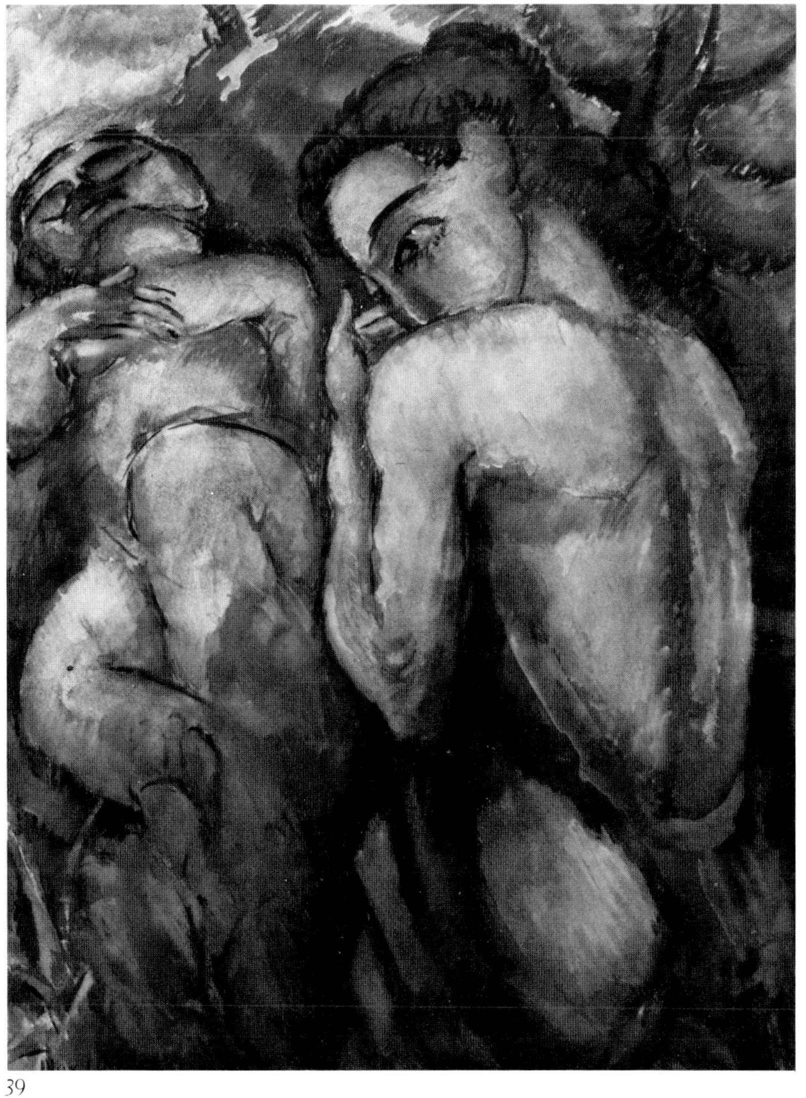

39

Tobey grew up in Wisconsin and Indiana, first studying art at the Art Institute of Chicago. After a brief stint as an illustrator, Tobey began to gravitate towards a teaching career and a more serious involvement in painting. In 1922 he gained two important experiences: a teaching job at the Cornish School in Seattle, and an introduction to the tenets of the Baha'i world faith, which was to shape his lifetime attitudes toward art. It was in Seattle that Tobey came to an understanding of abstract form through an investigation of Cubism, but almost immediately he extended this understanding to non-objective, philosophical principles associated with oriental aesthetics—an area of interest he was to explore throughout his life.

Not surprisingly, Tobey's art lagged behind his intellectual development. In the 1930s he began a somewhat nomadic existence as an artist/citizen of the world, living and working in various countries, storing up experiences. In time his art gravitated towards nonobjective renderings in a calligraphic style based upon Japanese aesthetics, which included an emphasis on brevity, concentration, simplicity, directness, and profundity. In a larger sense his work was bolstered by his Baha'i faith and a lifelong interest in Zen perception, which to him revealed a hidden beauty that lay beyond the rational mind.

Landscape, a small gouache, is indicative of Tobey's intense preoccupation with nature, which came as much from his boyhood memories as from his mature aesthetic. He once commented that the structure and process of nature interested him the most, the idea of "bringing the intangible into the tangible" (Seitz, p. 40). Here, in a small, evocative work, a broad *sumi* smoke of pale blue creates a sky as well as a mood; a tranquil, meditative study of nature that holds a fleeting moment, and carries it to our senses.

R.S.

Seitz, W. M. *Mark Tobey*. New York: Museum of Modern Art, 1962.

Mark Tobey. Washington: National Collection of Fine Arts, Smithsonian Institution, 1976.

MAX WEBER (1881–1961)

39. DRAPED FEMALE NUDE AND SLEEPING CHILD, 1911

Gouache on paper
24 1/4 x 18 5/8 (61.6 x 47.3)
Signed and dated lower left: *Max Weber 1911*
Williams College Museum of Art

Max Weber, perhaps the most important early American interpreter of Cubism, was born in Bialystok, Russia in 1881. Ten years later his family immigrated to America, settling in Brooklyn. From 1898 to 1901 Weber studied art at the Pratt Institute, where one of his teachers, Arthur Wesley Dow, emphasized the principles of design rather than the copying of models.

In 1905 Weber left for Paris, where he began painting at the Académie Julian and soon became a familiar face at the gatherings of the artistic vanguard. He spent a great deal of time in museums in Paris, Italy, Belgium, Spain and Holland. Eclectic in taste, he was interested in the art of the Orient and Africa, as well as the European masters and moderns. Primitive sculpture especially pleased him and had a lasting influence on his art, as did the work of Picasso and Cézanne.

In 1909 Weber returned to New York, where his first one-man show at the Haas Gallery brought a negative response. He soon gained the support of Alfred Stieglitz, however, who included him in a group exhibition of Young American Moderns at "291" in 1910. His painting and sculpture of the next few years show that along with being the first American to take up Cubism, he understood it better than perhaps any of his American peers.

Many of Weber's paintings from 1910 and 1911 reveal his preoccupation with the early Cubism of Picasso, as well as with sculpture and primitive art. The masklike face, twisted forms, and angular, sculptural treatment of the bodies in *Draped Female Nude with Sleeping Child* are, like his other nudes of this period, clear reactions to works by Picasso. Critics were shocked by the "grotesque" figures they saw at Weber's exhibition at "291" in January 1911. But there is beauty in the unself-conscious, graceful gestures of these nudes, and interest in Weber's solution to the problem of the handling of space. It is impossible to find one viewpoint; the planes are moved around so that we look frontally at the woman while at the same time we see the child moved into her plane from a perpendicular one. Our eyes travel around the canvas from one faceted shape to another, and this rhythm is complemented by the picture's soft grey, blue and green, which reveal Weber's sensitivity to color.

Draped Female Nude with Sleeping Child is important as one of the earliest American Cubist paintings. To pre-Armory Show New York this gouache was bizarre, but in retrospect the painting is striking for its early and sure understanding of Picasso and the direction modern art was taking.

T.W.

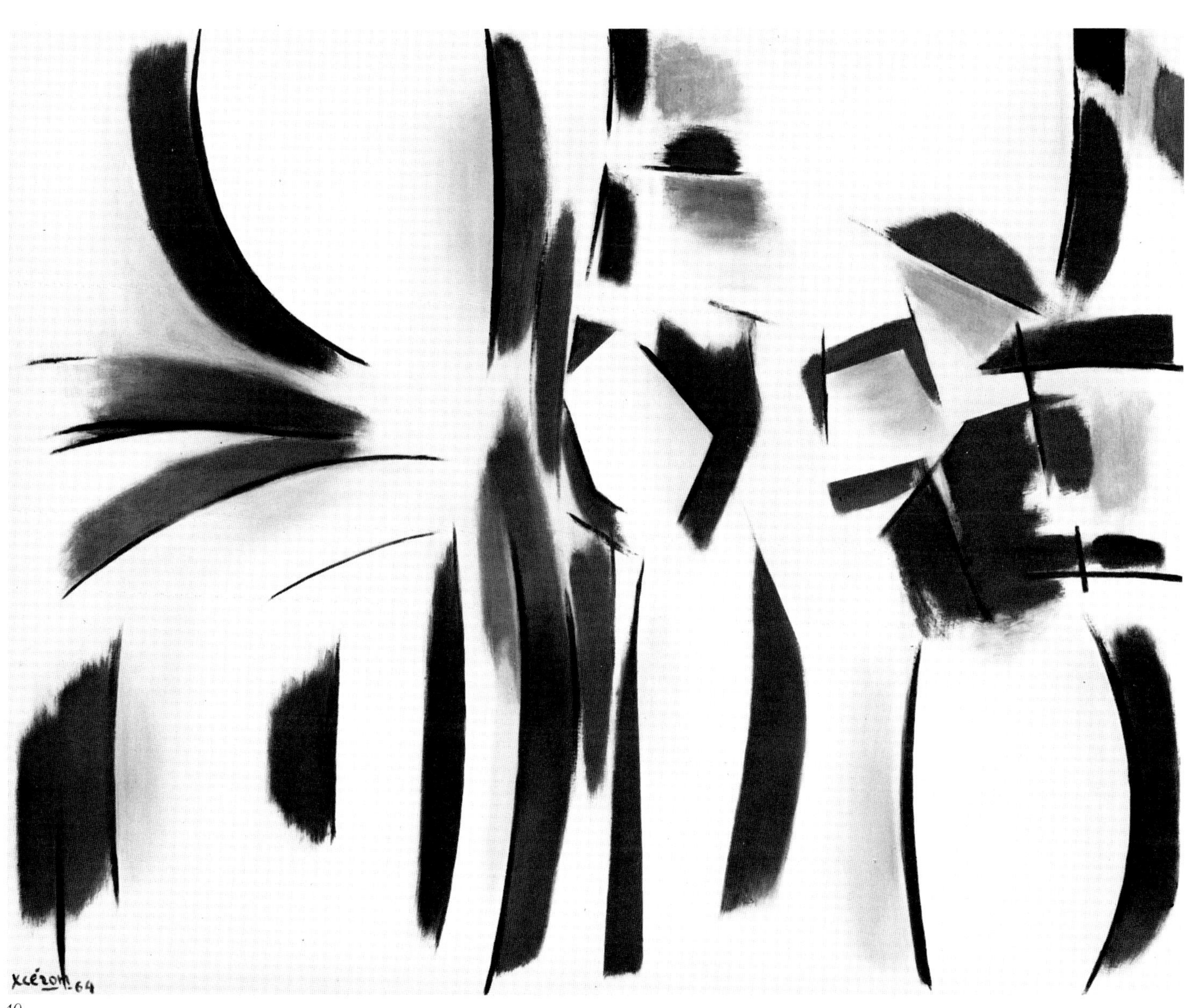

40

Goodrich, Lloyd. *Max Weber*. New York: The Whitney Museum of American Art and The MacMillan Co., 1949.

Max Weber Retrospective Exhibition. New York: Museum of Modern Art, 1930.

Werner, Alfred. *Max Weber*. New York: Watson-Guptill, 1975.

JEAN XCERON (1890–1967)

40. NO. 457, MORPHES, 1964

Oil on canvas
40⅛ x 51⅛ (101.9 x 129.9)
Signed and dated lower left: *Xceron '62*
Whitney Museum of American Art

Although not well-known today, Jean Xceron enjoyed a distinguished career as an artist. The son of a Greek blacksmith, Xceron came to America shortly before World War I and studied at the Corcoran Gallery of Art in Washington, D.C. There he was exposed, with a marked effect on his art, to Picasso and Cubism, as well as the art of Cézanne. Xceron subsequently moved to New York and became part of the Modernist art community, meeting members of the Stieglitz circle, going to the Whitney Studio Club exhibitions, and exhibiting with the New York Independents in 1921 and 1922.

In 1927 Xceron went to Paris, where he was first noticed as a young American critic sympathetic to modern art. By 1931, however, he was enjoying notoriety as a painter in his own right; he had his first one-man show at the Galerie de France, and struck up friendships with Mondrian, Arp, Léger, Van Doesburg, Masson and Hélion.

Xceron returned to America in 1927 as a successful and respected painter associated with Circle et Carré and Abstraction-Création groups. He became a much-admired member of the newly formed American Abstract Artists group, as well as one of the few modernist artists employed by the WPA to execute non-objective murals. Although by the 1940s Xceron was viewed as an "older" painter from an earlier era, his art nonetheless continued to command great respect.

Initially Xceron's paintings were well within the geometric abstractionist style of the 1930s and 1940s: rectangles, squares and circles arranged against a field of moderated color. By 1958, however, the geometric shapes were disappearing in favor of more organic forms which suggest the enlarged, evocative strokes of the Abstract Expressionist painters. Xceron painted *No. 457, Morphes* in 1964, by which time movement had become increasingly important in his paintings, and the colors stronger (although his watercolors and drawings remained comparatively placid and balanced). Executed when Xceron was over seventy, this painting seems a visual transliteration of ancient figures in a landscape, recalling, as the artist often did, the Greek sources of his Western artistic heritage.

R.S.

American Abstract Artists, ed. *The World of Abstract Art*. New York: Wittenborn, 1957.

Gianakoulis, Theodore. Contributors to American Culture: Jean Xceron." *Athene*, Chicago, vol. 8, 3 Autumn 1947, pp. 14–16.

Robbins, Daniel. *Jean Xceron*. New York: The Solomon R. Guggenheim Museum, 1965.